A Day-Tripper's Guide

AROUND TOKYO
VOL. 2

by John Turrent

The **Japan Times**, Ltd.

Published by The Japan Times, Ltd.

First edition: September, 1983

Jacket design by Atelier Hirata

Published by The Japan Times, Ltd.
5-4, Shibaura 4-chome, Minato-ku, Tokyo 108, Japan
ISBN4-7890-0218-7

Printed in Japan

FOREWORD

Tokyo is a city of many attractions, some of them well known, others hidden away on the backstreets. It is a delight to discover its local color in events like the Togenuki-Jizo fair in Sugamo, at places like Shibamata with its Yagiri ferry crossing the Edogawa River, or along hiking courses in the Okutama and Chichibu areas, near enough to be called Tokyo's back garden.

This book is a collection of articles which have appeared in The Japan Times or the Japan Times Weekly, introducing such places to foreign residents and visitors. It is a companion to "Around Tokyo Vol. 1." Together the two books provide plenty of material for people planning one-day and weekend trips. A comprehensive index covering both volumes is included at the end of this book.

The trips described in this second volume have been divided into three groups: "Hiking Courses," "Fairs" and "Leisure Trips." The first section covers hiking courses suitable for family and group outings, while "Fairs" introduces some less well-known temples and shrines in the area (which do not necessarily have to be visited only on fair day). Leisure trips extend farther afield, taking in several places like Nikko, Oshima and Matsumoto which require more than one day's trip. Fares and hotel prices have been included as a guide to expenses, but please remember that they are subject to change.

I would like to express my gratitude to Jonathan Lloyd-Owen, co-author of "Around Tokyo Vol. 1," for his editorial assistance on this second volume, and to the Aichi Prefecture Tokyo Office for permission to use the photograph which appears on page 114 and 116.

September, 1983

John Turrent

CONTENTS

Hiking Courses

iv

Guide Maps

Indexes

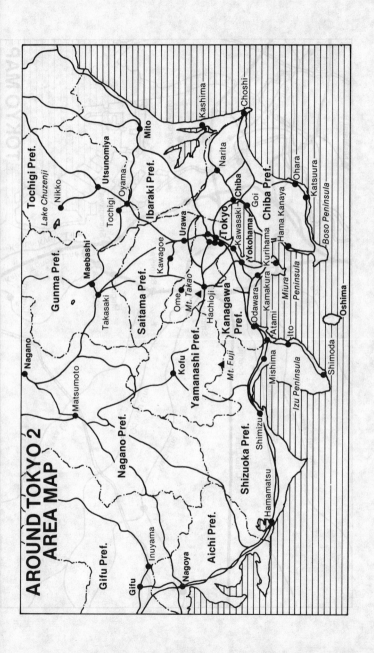

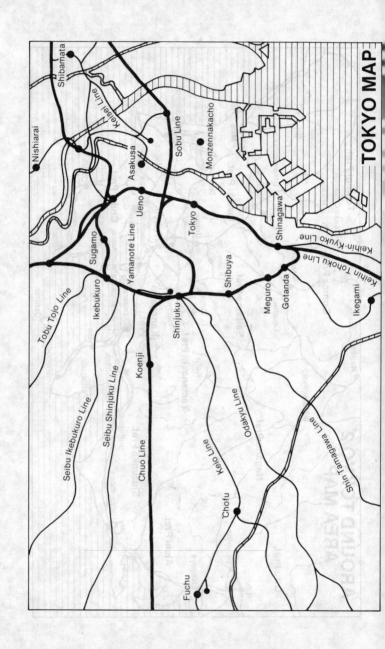

TOKYO MAP

Hiking Courses

Mount Takao and Beyond

高尾山、陣馬山

ONE of the first mountains which newcomers to Tokyo get to know is Mount Takao, in the western outskirts of the capital. It is easily reached by either the JNR Chuo Line from Shinjuku, or more cheaply by the privately-run Keio Line which also starts at Shinjuku.

Its convenient location, together with its modest 600-meter height, means that Mount Takao is a very popular day-trip destination. Cable car and lift services operate up the mountainside and there are six well laid-out courses around the mountaintop for hikers to choose from.

Less well-known is Mount Takao's neighbor to the northwest, Mount Jinba. It is possible to reach this 857-meter peak by one of two routes.

The easier and more direct approach is from Hachioji. Take the Keio Line to Keio-Hachioji Station, and then a bus from in front of this station to Jinbakogen-shita, the journey taking about 50 minutes and costing ¥520. Nishi-Tokyo buses leave at the rate of one an hour for Jinbakogen-shita, convenient times being 8:10 (8:30 on Sundays and holidays), 9:10 and 10:10 a.m. The next stop after Keio-Hachioji is JNR Hachioji Station (bus stop No. 1), so it is also possible to connect with the bus from the JNR Chuo Line.

On the way to Jinbakogen-shita there's a stop called Yuyake-Koyake. It is worth noting that this is where the popular Japanese song of the same name about the sunset originated. There is a monument to the fact in the precincts of the nearby shrine.

From the Jinbakogen-shita bus terminus, it takes an hour to walk up to Wada-toge pass. A few meters from the bus stop, you come to a small junction; turn right there for the pass.

At Wada-toge there are benches and tables at which to rest. The steep and at times slippery wooden steps leading up the slope from the pass take you to the top of Mount Jinba in about 40 minutes, and you are rewarded for your efforts with a fine view of Mount Fuji, some small stalls selling drinks and light snacks, and plenty of picnic space. And if you climb Mount Jinba in April, the cherry blossoms are an extra bonus.

The gently undulating route going down the far side of the mountain leads to Lake Sagami in about two hours. The hiking course ends at Yose Shrine, and the lake is five minutes across the expressway which runs past the shrine's entrance.

If you reach Lake Sagami by mid-afternoon, there's still time to take an excursion boat or go rowing on the lake before returning to Shinjuku from Sagamiko Station on the JNR Chuo Main Line.

The second and harder way to reach Mount Jinba is to go via Mount Takao. Take the Keio Line from Shinjuku to Takaosanguchi, and from there ascend the mountain by cable car. Look in at Mount Takao's Yakuoin Temple, then follow the route for Kobotoke-toge pass via Mount Shiroyama, which is easily identified by its prominent antenna tower. It should take about one hour from the temple to Mount Shiroyama, and then 20 minutes to Kobotoke-toge.

From Kobotoke-toge, the signposted course leads to Mount Kagenobu (727 meters), and from there to Meio-toge pass where there is a small drinks stall run by a very amiable old gentleman who spends his free time practicing gateball (a game similar to croquet).

At Meio-toge the course divides into two, one path going down to

Lake Sagami on the route from Mount Jinba in 80 minutes, and the other going up to the top of Mount Jinba in 40 minutes. From Mount Jinba, descend to Wada-toge and then follow the path down to the Jinbakogen-shita bus stop. Buses leave from there for Hachioji and Keio-Hachioji stations at 3:10, 4:10, 5:00 (5:10 on Sundays and holidays), 6:15 (6:30 on Sundays and holidays) and 6:55 p.m. (weekdays only).

The summit of Mount Jinba, with its white horse statue.

The two Mount Jinba courses, therefore, are as follows:

Easy course: Hachioji to Jinbakogen-shita by bus (50 min.); walk to Wada-toge (50 min.); walk to Mount Jinba (40 min.); walk to Meio-toge (30 min.); walk to Lake Sagami (80 min.); train from Sagamiko Station to Shinjuku by JNR Chuo Main Line (70 min.) Total walking time: 3 hours 30 min.

Hard course: Shinjuku to Takaosanguchi by Keio Line (45 min.); cable car up Mount Takao (5 min.); walk to Yakuoin Temple (20 min.); walk to Mount Shiroyama (60 min.); walk to Kobotoke-toge (20 min.); walk to Mount Kagenobu (30 min.); walk to Meio-toge (80 min.); walk to Mount Jinba (40 min.); walk to Jinbakogen-shita bus stop (70 min.); bus to Hachioji (50 min.). Total walking time: 5 hours 20 min.

Heading for Hatonosu Gorge

鳩ノ巣渓谷

GORGES are popular day-trip destinations, and the two main rivers flowing out of the Okutama hills in western Tokyo, the Tamagawa and Akikawa, have cut away plenty for the enjoyment of people living in the metropolitan area.

One of the best known and easiest to reach is Hatonosu Keikoku, on the Tamagawa river. A great fire in Edo (Tokyo) in 1657 indirectly gave the spot its name. In rebuilding the town, timber was required from the Okutama area, and people involved in the task of loading rafts with logs and sending them down the river noticed two pigeons *(hato)* which had set up their nest *(su)* in the area.

The two pigeons were apparently sighted every day, and consequently the valley came to be called Hatonosu Keikoku. It's a short walk from Hatonosu Station on the JNR Ome Line, 65 minutes from Tachikawa, and forms part of a pleasant hiking course when linked with Mount Mitake.

The course may be walked in either direction but for casual hikers Mount Mitake is recommended as the starting point. This has two advantages. One is that after ascending the mountain (929 meters) by cable car, the actual hike to the valley is nearly all downhill, and therefore not at all tiring.

The other advantage is that if you're going on a Sunday or national holiday, you can take the direct train from Shinjuku to Mitake, thereby avoiding the usual change at Tachikawa. At present direct trains leave Shinjuku on the JNR Chuo Line at 7:49, 8:16, 8:48 and 9:23 a.m. The train divides at Haijima, half of it going to Mitake and half to Musashi-Itsukaichi.

Take the bus from Mitake Station to Takimoto, from where it's a short walk up to the cable car which climbs almost to the top of the mountain in about six minutes.

For the hiking course, take the path leading to the left from the cable car terminus. One of the surprises of Mount Mitake is that this path, rather than leading immediately out into the hills, actually

5

takes you into a cluster of old buildings, some of them with fine thatched roofs.

The route leads to Mitake Shrine, but on the way you'll come to a sign pointing to the right and a path twisting off through more houses toward Hatonosu Keikoku. Follow this path round to one particularly splendid thatched-roof dwelling, and then branch off right again behind this house for the course to the gorge. The signs are in Japanese, so if you have any doubts, be sure to ask somebody the way.

From there it's a comfortable two-hour walk through cedar and cypress tunnels, the path emerging a couple of times to provide fine views of the Okutama hills. The only spot where you might go wrong is at Onara Toge, where the path divides. Turn right there, and continue straight on for Hatonosu.

As you approach the valley, you should be able to see a nearby rock face on which rock climbers can be seen practising their skills. Beyond this the path becomes a road, and crosses a bridge over the Tamagawa river.

After the bridge, take the path down to the left past souvenir shops and inns, and you'll see a suspension bridge spanning the gorge ahead of you. Once down by the river, you should be able to find a spot among the rocks where you can enjoy your lunch — and if you already consumed all you brought with you during the hike, the nearby Ishintei restaurant is noted for its home-made soba.

After replenishing your strength, you can cross the suspension bridge and take the short hiking course along the gorge as far as Shiromaru Dam. A U-turn across the river will take you back to Hatonosu Station along the Ome Kaido road in about 20 minutes.

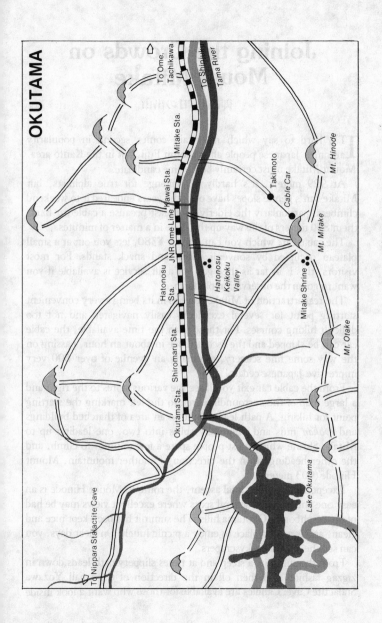

OKUTAMA

To Ome, Tachikawa

To Shinjuku

Tama River

Mitake Sta.

Kawai Sta.

JNR Ome Line

Hatonosu Sta.

Shiromaru Sta.

Okutama Sta.

Takimoto

Cable Car

Mt. Hinode

Mt. Mitake

Mitake Shrine

Mt. Otake

Hatonosu
Keikoku Valley

Lake Okutama

To Nippara Stalactite Cave

Joining the Crowds on Mount Mitake

御岳山、日の出山

IT'S hard to say which mountain comes second in popularity amongst Japanese people after Mount Fuji, but in the Kanto area, Mount Mitake must certainly be a prime candidate.

At 929 meters, it's hardly a challenge for true alpinists, but Mitake-san's gentle slopes have over the years endeared it to weekend climbers, particularly the elderly, not least because a cable car hauls them 830 meters of the way up the slope in a matter of minutes.

The cable car, which you can ride for ¥380, lets you out at a small plateau occupied by souvenir shops and snack stands. For most visitors, this is as far as they go, but a lift service is available if you want to go up the observation platform.

The real attraction of Mitake-san lies in its being a very convenient starting point for several excellent, easily navigated and not too difficult hiking courses. For those with the time available, the cable car can be skipped and the ascent made in about an hour, passing on the way some fine scenery, especially an avenue of over 600 very impressive Japanese cedars.

From the cable car exit you'll see the various stores to the right and a large map of the surrounding area to the left marking the starting point for hiking. A path leads round to an area of thatched buildings and *ryokan* inns and eventually splits into two, one leading up to Mitake Shrine which most people spare a few minutes to climb, and the other heading off in the direction of another mountain, Mount Hinode (903 meters).

Except for a steepish final ascent, the route to Mount Hinode is an easy one and provides several spots where excellent views may be had of the neighboring Okutama hills. The summit has been kept nice and clean, and is a good place to enjoy a picnic lunch. On clear days, you can see the Shinjuku skyscrapers.

From the summit, a steep and at times slippery path leads down in zigzag fashion and then off in the direction of the small Yozawa Stalactite Cave. Candles are available for those who want a look inside but be warned, it's dark, wet and a tight squeeze at times.

The path leaving the lodge runs down to meet the Yozawa River, and a 20-minute walk along the road running parallel to it brings you to the Kami-Yozawa bus stop for Musashi-Itsukaichi Station.

All the hiking courses in these hills are clearly signposted, but mainly in Japanese. If you have any doubts, ask one of the nature-loving, berry-picking, bird-watching hikers who pass by.

Mitake-san is reached by bus from Mitake Station. On Sundays and holidays, trains run direct to Mitake from Shinjuku. Otherwise, change onto the Ome Line at Tachikawa. Alternatively, the Seibu Shinjuku Line has trains going to Haijima, which is near Mitake on the Ome Line. Buses for the Takimoto cable car station leave from just outside Mitake Station (turn left at the exit) and the fare is ¥170.

Course: Shinjuku to Mitake Station by JNR Chuo and Ome lines (about 90 minutes); bus to cable car (10 minutes); cable car ascent (6 minutes) or walk to summit (about 60 minutes); from Mitake-san to Mitake Shrine (25 minutes); from shrine to Mount Hinode (45 minutes); from Mount Hinode to Yozawa Cave (40 minutes); from cave to bus stop (40 minutes); bus to Musashi-Itsukaichi Station (35 minutes); back to Shinjuku by JNR Itsukaichi and Chuo lines (about 70 minutes).

Spelunking Around Tokyo

日原鐘乳洞

A S well as being famous for its range of hills and mountains, the Okutama and Chichibu area to the west of Tokyo is also renowned for its many caves, and especially the stalactite caverns which have formed in the limestone rock of the region.

With temperatures inside these caverns staying between 11 and 13 degrees C throughout the year, they provide a welcome respite from winter chill and summer heat. While the surrounding mountains and gorges of the district have their off-seasons, caves attract explorers all the year round with their fascinating stalactite and stalagmite rock formations.

Nippara Cave

The biggest and most visited stalactite cave in the Kanto region is Nippara Shonyudo, or Nippara Cave, a 30-minute ride by Nishi Tokyo bus from Okutama Station at the end of the JNR Ome Line from Tachikawa.

The bus leaves from in front of the station. On weekdays it goes as far as the Nippara Shonyudo bus stop near the entrance to the cave, but on Sundays and national holidays, in order to avoid traffic congestion on the narrow road, it stops at Higashi-Nippara bus stop. From there it's a 25-minute walk over the remaining distance. Don't be put off — the road goes alongside the Nippara River and passes some fine scenery.

The Nippara Cave is over 500 meters deep and visitors can go down and explore to about 280 meters. Entrance is ¥300. A lighted course directs you around the cavern, up and down between the "old" and "new" parts, and past various rock shapes. The largest stalagmite stands two meters high and is called the Byakui Kannon because of its resemblance to statues of the Goddess of Mercy. It is said that stalagmites take about 400 years to grow 3 cm, which means that the Byakui Kannon has taken well over 26,000 years to reach its present height.

Just beyond the Nippara Cave there are also popular facilities for trout fishing, and a large car park is located nearby for those who want to drive out. The cave is open throughout the year every day from 8 a.m. until 4:30 p.m. Tel.: 04288-3-2099. Inquiries should be made in Japanese.

A Buddhist statue inside Nippara Cave.

Kurasawa Cave

This cave is located quite near the Nippara Shonyudo, but fewer people seem to visit it. This is possibly because it hasn't been fitted out with electric lighting for the benefit of tourists, although some might find entering a cave armed with a torch an added excitement.

Entrance to the Kurasawa Cave is ¥200, and about 180 meters can be explored. It is a 30-minute walk from Kurasawa bus stop on the same bus route which connects Okutama and Nippara Cave. It is open every day from 9 a.m. to 5 p.m., but if you're going in winter, telephone beforehand to check. Tel.: 04288-3-2653.

Odake Cave

There are three well-known caves in the Itsukaichi area, and Odake Shonyudo is the largest with a 300-meter course going to a depth of over 100 meters. Stairways and lighting have been installed in this cave, which was discovered as recently as 1961.

Odake Cave is open from 9 a.m. to 5 p.m. every day, and entrance is ¥300. It is a 30-minute walk from Odakeguchi bus stop, the penultimate stop on the Nishi Tokyo bus route from Musashi-Itsukaichi Station to Kami-Yozawa, the journey taking 35 minutes.

Mitsugo Cave

The second cave in the area is Mitsugo Cave, discovered in 1970 and a 15-minute walk to the west from Mitsugo Shonyudo Iriguchi bus stop on the same Nishi Tokyo bus route. The 100-meter-long course runs 50 meters deep. Entrance is ¥500, and the cave is open from 9 a.m. to 5 p.m.

Yozawa Cave

The third cave in the Itsukaichi area is Yozawa Shonyudo, or Yozawa Cave, which is a small cave with a narrow course of about 70 meters in length. Entrance is ¥200, and you receive a candle to help you around — but beware, it's a tight squeeze in places. This cave is particularly popular with hikers who stop off while doing the Mt. Mitake to Mt. Hinode hiking course. It's a 30-minute walk north from Kami-Yozawa bus stop on the same Nishi Tokyo bus route from Musashi-Itsukaichi Station.

Hashitate Cave

One more cave worth noting is Hashitate Shonyudo, or Hashitate Cave, located in the precincts of Hashitate Temple in Chichibu.The entrance to the cave is located just behind the temple's Kannon-do statue, and the exit leads back into the temple compound. The temple, which is the 28th stage on the Chichibu pilgrimage course, is a 10-minute walk from Urayamaguchi Station on the Chichibu Dentetsu Railway.

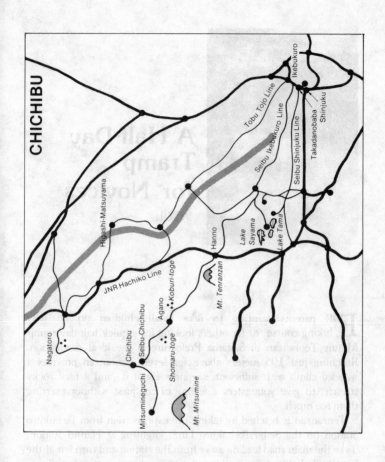

A Half-Day
Tramp
for Novices
天覧山

FOR parents wanting to take small children on an easy hiking course, or for others looking for a quick half-day tramp, Mount Tenranzan in Saitama Prefecture is the ideal destination. Reaching just 195 meters above sea level, Tenranzan provides a wooded climb with sufficient steepness about it, and a final rocky stretch, to give youngsters a feeling of conquest without exerting them too much.

Tenranzan is reached by taking the express train from Ikebukuro Station on the Seibu Ikebukuro Line, alighting at Hanno Station. Take the main road leading away from the station and turn left at the first traffic lights. Keep walking along this shopping street until you reach the large white Chuo Komin Kaikan building.

From the right side of this building, a road leads down to the Naguri River (which seems to change its name to the Iruma River somewhere in the vicinity). Boating, fishing, picnicking and even swimming can be enjoyed there.

For Tenranzan, keep heading along the road in a northwesterly direction for about 10 more minutes until you reach the Tenranzan-shita bus stop, and the road leading right from there takes you up to

Noninji Temple, at the foot of the mountain. It's worth stopping for a rest there to see the main hall, rebuilt in 1936, and the pleasant Japanese-style garden behind it. The original main hall was burnt down in an 1868 battle related to the Meiji Restoration.

From the temple entrance, the road going off to the right leads to the mountain path and eventually to the top in about 20 minutes. Just below the summit, the path splits into two, one branch going straight to the top, the other taking the climber round past 16 small Buddhist statues and up a slightly rocky course to the top. The statues date from the period of the fifth Tokugawa shogun, Tsuneyoshi (1648-1709), and were built in gratitude after prayers at Noninji for the shogun's recovery from illness were "answered."

The slope leading from the righthand side of the stall on the top of Tenranzan goes down to an open field from where the path to the left heads back toward Hanno Station, and that to the right toward Mount Tonosuyama, standing 271 meters high and offering somewhat better views of the surrounding countryside and hills than does Tenranzan. The wooded path winding up to the summit shouldn't provide any problems, even for small children.

Just before the summit, the path divides into two, the right one being the steeper Otoko-zaka, and the other being Onna-zaka, which passes the small Amagori Pond.

The summit of Mount Tenranzan —
even kindergarten children can make it.

15

From the top of Tonosuyama, retrace your steps a short way and then take the path to the right, which leads down the mountainside and eventually comes out at the main Naguri Kaido road. Walk along the road to the right, and you'll soon find the bus stop for Hanno Station. If you have enough time before a bus comes (there are about two an hour), cross the road and you can walk down to the river.

Course: Seibu Ikebukuro Station to Hanno (50 minutes by express); from Hanno Station to Chuo Komin Kaikan (20-minute walk); from there to Noninji Temple (10 minutes); from there to top of Tenranzan (20 minutes); from Tenranzan to Tonosuyama (about 45 minutes); from summit to bus stop (about 25 minutes); bus to Hanno Station (10 minutes).

Alternatively, Tenranzan is also the starting point for the Oku-Musashi Nature Trail. From the open area midway up Tenranzan, the path to the right leads to Koma Pass, crossing National Route 299 and the Seibu Line on the way. Eventually you reach the Koma River and Koma Station, from where express trains reach Ikebukuro in about one hour.

Up and Down to the Kuroyama Falls

顔振峠

KOBURI-toge in Saitama Prefecture has the very best of credentials, for it was from none other than the great 12th century warrior Minamoto Yoshitsune that the peak got its name.

Apparently, when Yoshitsune made the ascent he spent so much time turning this way and that to admire the view that inevitably some wit came up with the name Koburi, which means something like "head-turning."

Koburi-toge is reached from Agano Station on the Seibu Ikebukuro Line, 70 minutes by express from Ikebukuro. Turn right out of the station, walk down to the road below, and follow the road to the right until you reach Agano Bridge. With the bridge behind you, turn left, and then right where the road forks at a bridge and you take off along a mountain path which soon starts zigzagging up.

After a steady 50-minute climb you come out at an asphalt road and two teahouses. This is the *toge* or pass — altitude about 450 meters. Pause for a rest there, then cross the road and make the final assault on the 500-meter peak.

Having enjoyed, or (if the weather's bad) imagined, the views which so delighted Yoshitsune, return to the nearer teahouse and follow the path going off to the right for the three waterfalls of Kuroyama. After a 40-minute walk downhill you reach a road. Turn left for the falls, but keep a lookout on your left for an old *gassho-zukuri* farm-house transplanted from Shirakawa in Gifu Prefecture and worth a short diversion.

Back on the road, the falls are not far away. Eventually you come to a junction with a large tourist map of the area on the corner. The road to the right leads to a bus stop from where a Tobu bus will take you to Ogose Station on the Tobu Tojo Line if, after seeing the falls, you wish to return to Ikebukuro.

The road to the left leads past a number of inns and shops, and a small bridge on the left which goes to Tengu, or Goblin, waterfall, the largest of the three and also the most picturesque, hidden away among the cliffs.

Stay on along the road and you come to the other two waterfalls, or rather one double waterfall, the upper part known as the Otaki, or male, waterfall, and the lower part as the Metaki, or female, waterfall.

At this point you might want to call it a day and return to the bus stop, but if you have the time and energy, you can hike to Takayama Fudo Temple. To do this, retrace your steps from the falls, watching out for a path which goes up and off to the left. There is a signpost, but it's almost illegible and easily missed, so ask directions at one of the shops if in doubt.

It's a good idea to purchase some *ichiri-ame*, honey candies which are popular souvenirs of Kuroyama and are so-called because one candy is supposed to last a full *ri*'s hiking, a *ri* being equal to nearly 2.5 miles. A bag costs ¥180.

Once on the course, you face a route that is quite breathtaking both for its cedar forest scenery and its steepness. After a one-hour climb you reach a road, where you should turn right. Follow the road for about 15 minutes and you come to a sharp bend, by the righthand corner of which is a path going up to another road, and then up again to a 770-meter-high observation point. In the center is the small "inner hall" of Takayama Fudo.

After a well-deserved rest, return to the bottom of the path, turn the corner and head down left for the main temple, the red roof of which soon comes into view. A large, commanding structure, Takayama Fudo was founded in 654.

From there, go down the temple steps and turn right for the route which leads to Nishi-Agano Station, one stop along from Agano Station. Turn left at the road, and follow it under the railway line, then left to the station.

If you attempt the whole Koburi-toge — Kuroyama Waterfalls-Takayama Fudo course, be sure to make an early start, and allow yourself at least one hour to descend from the temple before dark falls.

And a Little Rock Climbing

正丸峠

SHOMARU-toge pass is the starting point for several hiking courses in the hills to the west of Tokyo, and one of the best for a day trip is that linking the pass with nearby Mount Izugatake.

To reach Shomaru-toge take the Seibu Ikebukuro Line from Ikebukuro and alight at Shomaru Station. If you're on the Seibu Shinjuku Line, take the train as far as Tokorozawa and change onto the Ikebukuro Line. It takes about 90 minutes from Ikebukuro to Shomaru by express or limited express.

From Shomaru Station, go down the steps to the right and follow the road through a tunnel under the railway line. Then enjoy a pleasant walk by the side of a stream, and after about 20 minutes' gentle climb you reach a mountain path.

A few more minutes and you come to a small and enshrined Bato-Kannon statue, and the path there divides into two. The course to the left leads directly up to Izugatake, but it's best to avoid this one and take the route to the right for Shomaru-toge, about 40 minutes' walk away.

At one point the path divides, with a branch going up to the right for the Shomaru-toge Garden House restaurant and camp site. Otherwise it's a problem-free climb except for the very last stretch where a rope is waiting to help you haul yourself up.

There is actually a road leading up to this 636-meter-high pass, so it comes as a bit of a disappointment to be greeted after an exerting climb by the sound of cars and motorbikes. Never mind, though, because the path leading off to the left soon takes you away from all this and back into the hills.

At first the view is limited by the surrounding foliage, but after a while the panorama opens up to take in both near and distant mountains as you approach Mount Kodaka (730 meters). There are benches here for those who want to take their lunches before tackling the final goal — Mount Izugatake — which rises nearby.

The ascent of Izugatake is not as difficult as it appears. Follow the path from Mount Kodaka and, after another stretch where a rope has been laid to help you up, it eventually splits into the Otoko-zaka and the Onna-zaka hill paths. The latter route is the easier of the two. Just follow the path round and a steady winding climb brings you to the 851-meter summit.

For those who really want to test their climbing skills, however, there is a chain waiting to help you up the rocky face of the Otoko-zaka side. Whichever route you take, the summit welcomes you with a fine 360-degree view of the surrounding mountains.

After a leisurely rest there, take the Onna-zaka route down to the foot of the rock course, and then the path leading down opposite you for Shomaru Station. After a while, the path comes to an end and you have to make a steep descent down a sandy slope which bears the mark of more backsides than footprints.

From the foot of the slope, you're on a path again and have an easy walk to the Bato-Kannon statue, and thence to Shomaru Station using the same road by which you came.

Course: Ikebukuro to Shomaru Station (90 min. by Seibu Ikebukuro Line); 25-min. walk to Bato-Kannon; 40-min. walk to Shomaru-toge pass; 35-min. walk to Mount Kodaka; 25-min. walk to Izugatake peak; 50-min. descent to Bato-Kannon, and 20-min. walk back to Shomaru Station.

History and Nature on Mt. Mitsumine

三峰山

SATURDAY. Clear and sunny weather.

6:50 a.m.: Leave Seibu Ikebukuro Station on the special Chichibu Express for Seibu-Chichibu. Fare ¥540 plus ¥430 for special express ticket. Seats must be reserved, but there is plenty of space on this early train.

8:11 a.m.: Arrive at Seibu-Chichibu Station and walk the short distance to Hanabatake Station on the Chichibu Dentetsu Railway.

8:21 a.m.: Take the local train for Mitsumineguchi Station, arriving at 8:42 a.m. Fare ¥230.

8:50 a.m.: Catch a bus which leaves from outside Mitsumineguchi Station and alight at Owa, the journey taking just 15 minutes. From here it's a short walk to the ropeway station, but . . . too early! There is an hour to wait before the first ropeway run up the 1,100-meter mountain. Choose to eat a very early lunch rather than walking to the top, because the climb would take at least a couple of hours.

10:15 a.m.: Take the ropeway up the mountainside, reaching the terminus in eight minutes, and then set off on the Mitsumine course which includes Mitsumine Shrine, a local museum, a Visitor Center and several other attractions. The brightly colored main hall of the shrine dates from 1661, and the impressive *zuijinmon* gate, a short distance away, was built in 1792. The museum contains displays related to the shrine and Mount Mitsumine, while the Visitor Center exhibits models and photographs of the Chichibu landscape and natural environment.

Before starting, it's worth picking up a guide map at the ropeway station, because on the back of it you can stamp the tourist motif of each spot you visit, including the small post office found in the precincts of the shrine. It makes a nice souvenir to take back home.

12:30 p.m.: Arrive back at the ropeway terminus after completing the circular course, and then set off on the route for Lake Chichibu. The path leads off in the opposite direction to the shrine, and after a while branches off down to the right for the lake.

The lantern-lined path leading to the zuijinmon gate near Mitsumine Shrine.

1:10 p.m.: Emerge at the toll gate on the mountainside road. Keep on in the same direction, following the path down the mountain. After 25 minutes, pass the remains of an old charcoal kiln built into the hillside, and 10 minutes later emerge at the road again, and am treated to an excellent view of Mount Kumotori, the largest mountain in Tokyo at 2,017 meters, and Mount Shiraiwa. Mount Mitsumine actually gets its name from the fact that three nearby peaks tower above it, these two plus Myohogadake.

Follow the road down for a short distance, and the hiking course can be seen leading off to the right.

2:25 p.m.: Arrive at the road which runs by Lake Chichibu, with a narrow and swaying suspension bridge visible to the left. Cross this bridge, turn left, and walk for about 15 minutes until coming to a small waterfall. This is a good spot for a picnic.

After a rest here, return to the bridge, and then keep on along the path which leads round Lake Chichibu. Boating facilities are available on the lake in season. To return to Mitsumineguchi Station, cross to the other side of the lake by bridge and head in the direction of Futase Dam. The Lake Chichibu bus stop is on the opposite side of the dam.

Course: Seibu-Ikebukuro Station — Seibu-Chichibu Station — Hanabatake Station — Mitsumineguchi Station — bus to Owa — ropeway up Mount Mitsumine — Mitsumine Shrine — museum — Visitor Center — ropeway terminus — hiking course for Lake Chichibu — back to Mitsumineguchi Station by bus.

Mount Mitsumine is also the starting point for two-day hikes to Mount Kumotori, or one-day hikes to Mount Myohogadake. Follow the path from the ropeway terminus which leads to the shrine, but instead of turning off for the latter, keep on going for the entrance to the Kumotori course.

After continuing along this path for about 30 minutes, you'll reach a torii arch. Pass under this arch and keep on walking for about 15 minutes, then begin a steep 20-minute climb to the top of Mount Myohogadake (1,332 meters), where you'll find the inner sanctuary of Mitsumine Shrine. Return by the same route to the ropeway terminus, and thence back to Mitsumineguchi Station by ropeway and bus.

Try Your Hand at Farming

藤野園芸ランド

THE period from September through mid-October is the season of the year for chestnut gathering, while sweet potatoes are ready for digging up between September and late November. *Sansai* (edible wild plants) and strawberries are available from about April to July, potatoes from May to June, *tomorokoshi* (corn) in July and August, and mushrooms all the year round.

That is the harvesting schedule at Fujino Engei Land, a tourist center made up of five small villages in the northern part of Kanagawa Prefecture, near the more well-known attractions of Lake Sagami and Sagamiko Picnic Land. With mushrooms, chestnuts and sweet potatoes in abundance, autumn is the best time to visit and try your hand at a little farming — that's right, the back-bending task of digging up the spuds is left to visitors themselves, who pay for what they harvest.

To reach the site, take the JNR Chuo Line from Shinjuku and alight at Fujino Station, which is a couple of stops after Takao. Be careful, because express trains don't stop there.

The road from Fujino Station leads down to a busy main road, where if you turn left and walk for a few minutes (going right at the fork), you come to a large arch announcing the entrance to Fujino Engei Land.

A better way to approach the *hatake,* or fields, however, is to turn right at the main road, and then left where it leads down to Bentenbashi bridge across the Sagami River. Take in the view, cross the bridge and you can turn either left (leading to the Engei Land Center), or right to follow the hiking course.

Turning right and following the road through small fields and chestnut groves, you eventually come to a wide road. Keep on until you come to an arch marking the start of the course. The road beyond passes Ishitateo Shrine on the right, with its two giant cedars standing side by side.

A little farther along you'll see some stone steps leading up to the left into the wooded hill. After coming out at an observation platform with benches and tables, follow the path up through an oak forest (it's quite steep but a chain makes the going easy) and over Nagura Pass.

When you emerge at an asphalt road, turn right and walk downhill a short while until you see another arch on the left with stone steps leading up, a continuation of the hiking course. Follow the path and it eventually brings you round to the Engei Land Center, where among other things archery and barbecue facilities are provided, and you can get information about vegetable-gathering.

From the road below this center, turn right and a 20-minute walk brings you to the Fujino Flower Garden, with its large greenhouse noted for its cyclamen plants in November. Boating and fishing facilities on the river are also popular in this area, and nearby there is a bonsai garden.

To return to Fujino Station, follow the road leading away from the Flower Garden and over Akiyama River via Akigawa Bridge. Then take the road to the left along the embankment and cross Sagami River by Hizure Bridge, near where the two rivers join. This brings you to the main entrance arch mentioned above, and a short walk to the left is the station.

The hiking course itself takes about three hours, but remember that extra time will be needed for any harvesting you might wish to do. For those planning to barbecue as well, it's best to telephone ahead. The number is 0426-87-3749.

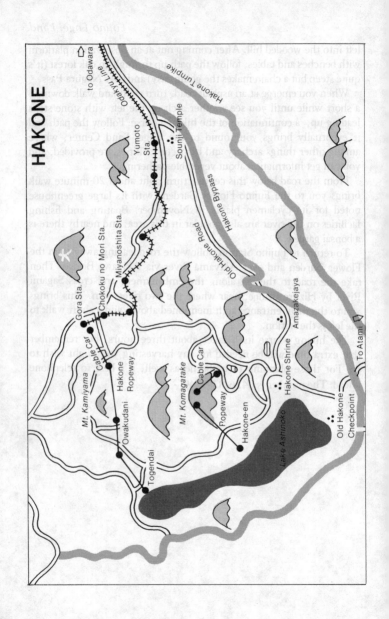

Where Daimyo Lords Once Walked

箱根旧街道

THE Old Hakone Road which in Edo days linked Mishima and Odawara has long been replaced as a main traffic artery by the Hakone Bypass and Hakone Turnpike, but its retirement has not meant atrophy. In place of the *daimyo* processions of olden times there is today a steady flow of hikers' boots, for the section between Moto-Hakone and Hakone-Yumoto has become a popular weekend course.

Moto-Hakone is reached in about one hour by bus from outside Odawara Station (bus stop No. 3, fare ¥870). Before setting off on the walk, it's worth visiting the Hakone Checkpoint and its museum.

Alighting from the bus by the shore of Lake Ashinoko, walk to the avenue of cedar trees which you'll see ahead of you, and follow it until you emerge at a road. Cross the road, pass through the car park, and eventually you'll come to the Hakone Checkpoint.

This checkpoint was set up in 1619 and remained in operation until 1869, its main function being to control the movement of the population and thereby ensure the power of the Tokugawa Shogunate.

No one could pass through without a special travel permit, and it is said that if a woman gave birth to a child before reaching the barrier, she would have to return to Edo to obtain a new permit before being allowed through. The only exceptions were entertainers, who were permitted to pass after demonstrating their talents to wary checkpoint officials.

The Hakone Checkpoint was reconstructed in 1965, and the nearby museum opened in the same year with various items on display related to the checkpoint and the old Hakone route.

Return to the bus stop and continue on to the large red torii arch ahead of you. Beyond lies Hakone Shrine, while the road to the right takes you to the starting point of the hiking course.

The present *ishidatami* paving was mostly laid in the 1860s, but there are short sections which remain from earlier days. The first stretch ends at the Amazakejaya tea house, where, like travelers of yore, you can rest and freshen up with a snack of rice cakes and sweet sake.

Look in at the adjacent Kyukaido Shiryokan museum, then continue along the Old Hakone Road until you reach a pedestrian bridge. Cross over, and the path going down to the right leads to another section of old ishidatami paving. Eventually you come to a roadside tea-house. Follow the road and wind round the Nanamagari, a series of seven consecutive sharp bends.

After the last bend, more steps go down to the right and on to more of the old road. Follow this and you emerge at the village of Hatajuku, famous for its *yosegi* marquetry. There are several places, including the central Yosegi Kaikan, where you can observe craftsmen at work and buy souvenirs.

Take the main village road and, leaving the houses behind, you come to yet more ishidatami on the left, after which you come out at the road again near the Hatsudensho-mae bus stop. Descend the steps there and take the path over the stream and on to the road again. From there, turn right, and it's a straight walk to Hakone-Yumoto, passing Shogenji and Sounji temples on the way. Odakyu "Romance Car" special express trains run from Hakone-Yumoto to Shinjuku in about 90 minutes.

Course: Hakone Checkpoint (15-min. walk) — Moto-Hakone (30-min. walk) — Amazakejaya tea house (60-min. walk) — Hatajuku (90-min. walk) — Hakone-Yumoto. This course is nearly all downhill. The route from Hakone-Yumoto in the direction of Moto-Hakone involves several uphill stretches and would take longer.

Getting Off to a Swinging Start

箱根

SATURDAY. Cloudy, with sunny spells.

7:37 a.m.: Depart from Shinjuku Station on an Odakyu Line express train bound for Odawara. Fare ¥500.

9:12 a.m.: Arrive at Odawara Station.

9:26 a.m.: Leave Odawara Station on the Hakone Tozan Tetsudo railway for Gora. The fare is ¥450. On the way the train passes Chokoku no Mori, and some sculptures of the open-air museum can be seen from the window.

10:14 a.m.: Arrive at Gora Station and switch to the cable car for Mount Sounzan. The ride up the 1,137-meter-high mountain takes 10 minutes. Then change to the ropeway for a trip across the Owakudani Valley (fare: ¥550), an uncomfortable ride with 12 people crammed into a small "gondola." Nobody can move because of the squeeze, and the windows quickly steam up and obscure the surrounding scenery — although this is probably just as well, because the valley is wide and deep. Not for the fainthearted!

11:08 a.m.: At Owakudani we alight from the gondola, which then continues its journey to Togendai on Lake Ashinoko. Visitors to Owakudani are met by the smell of sulphurous fumes which pour out

Volcanic fumes fill the air at Owakudani Valley.

29

of the earth here and create clouds of white smoke in the sky. A short walk from the gondola station are some souvenir shops, and beyond, a spot where people can observe the volcanic fumes and bubbling water more closely. On sale here are *kuro-tamago,* or blackened eggs, which have been boiled in the sulphurous steam. Five eggs cost ¥400, and one egg is supposed to add seven years to your life, so it's a cheap investment!

Noon: Set off on the hiking course for Mount Komagatake, entrance to which is reached by taking the path which starts just to the left of the souvenir shops as you approach them. After a short while there is a sign pointing to the course which leads up to the left.

1:05 p.m.: Reach a spot where the path divides into two after a steep climb and a rest for a snack on the way. The path to the left leads back to Mount Sounzan. Keep on going up for Mount Kamiyama and Mount Komagatake.

1:40 p.m.: Reach a small torii archway marking the way to the small shrine on top of Mount Kanmurigatake. From there, follow the path up to the top of Mount Kamiyama, the highest spot on the course at 1,438 meters.

2:20 p.m.: Follow the path down from Mount Kamiyama toward Mount Komagatake. After 25 minutes reach an open area, and then a junction. Follow the path to the right for Komagatake. There are occasionally steep descents on the way.

3:10 p.m.: Arrive at Mount Komagatake, but the mist is very heavy. The paved path to the right leads to a ropeway for Hakone-en, and that to the left leads to a cable car station. On the way to the cable car, the path passes the small Hakone Mototsumiya Shrine, a branch of the main Hakone Shrine. According to the priest here, the 1,327-meter mountain is often shrouded in mist, but when it rises, the views are spectacular. On a couple of occasions each year, he said, even Sunshine 60 in Ikebukuro can be seen.

3:45 p.m.: Take the cable car down to the foot of the mountain, and catch a bus for Odawara at 4 p.m. (¥300 for the cable car, ¥750 for the bus). From Odawara, catch the Odakyu "Romance Car" express back to Shinjuku.

("Free passes" for Hakone can be bought at any Odakyu railway station. The pass, which costs ¥3,800 from Shinjuku, gives unlimited access to trains, buses and cable cars in the area.)

Keep Your Eyes off the Garbage

大山

MOUNT Oyama belongs to the Tanzawa range in Kanagawa Prefecture. The foot of the 1,246-meter peak can be reached in an hour and a half from Shinjuku. An Odakyu Line express train gets you to Isehara Station in an hour, and the bus leaving from the north exit reaches Oyama Cable bus stop, its terminus, in just over 20 minutes. The train fare is ¥350 and the bus fare ¥170.

The road leading from the bus stop up to the cable car station is lined with eateries offering refreshing tofu dishes and souvenir shops selling popular Oyama spinning tops.

At the cable car station the crowds thin out, most people electing to take the six-minute cable ride halfway up the slope, others opting for the hiking course, which covers the same distance in about 40 minutes. There are two walking routes, the Onna-zaka (female slope) and the Otoko-zaka (male slope), the latter being the longer and harder of the two. Midway up Onna-zaka is Daisanji Temple, better known as Oyama Fudo. This can also be reached from the cable car's Fudo-mae station.

Next is Oyama Afuri Shrine, the last stop on the cable car route. Like the temple, this shrine was originally founded in the year 755, and its "upper half" is to be found on the summit. For those who forget their picnic lunches, it's a good idea to have a bowl of *soba* or *oden* at one of the eating places at the foot of the steps leading to the shrine before continuing the journey to the top. And don't miss the nearby Nijuno-taki waterfall.

There are, in fact, three routes from the shrine to the summit, but most people take the direct one going up from the left of the shrine building. It's not an easy climb, the path being strewn with artificial stone steps which make it hard on the feet — stout shoes are recommended.

A total of 28 numbered posts mark the way, with resting places at posts 12 and 16, and the ascent takes about an hour and a half. Wild birds and flowers and several commanding views reward your efforts.

31

Steps leading up to Afuri Shrine on Mount Oyama.

Another pleasant aspect of the climb is the friendly greetings one receives from people coming in the opposite direction, although in the case of Mount Oyama one wishes they wouldn't leave quite so much rubbish behind to greet your arrival on the summit. The general scruffiness contrasts with the splendid scenery. On a clear day, Enoshima and Mount Fuji are visible.

About 10 minutes down from the summit a path branches off to the right and leads to Yabitsu Pass in about 50 minutes. Buses from the pass are few and far between, so it's worthwhile continuing your hike round to Minoge along a pleasant mountain path. From Minoge, a Kanagawa Chuo bus takes you to Ohatano Station on the Odakyu Line in about 25 minutes.

Course: Shinjuku to Isehara Station by Odakyu Line (55 min.); Isehara to Oyama Cable Station by Kanagawa Chuo bus (20 min.); from there to Afuri Shrine by cable car (6 min.) or walking (about 40 min.); from there to summit (1 hour 30 min.); from summit to Yabitsu Pass (1 hour); from there to Minoge (50 min.); from Minoge to Ohatano Station by bus (25 min.). The course can, of course, be taken in the opposite direction, starting from Minoge. For those descending Mount Oyama, note that the last cable car down is at 5 p.m.

A Seaside Hiking Course

剣崎

AFTER summer is over and the tide of holidaymakers draws back for another year, the seaside becomes the preserve of fishermen and hikers. One of the places where they congregate is down on the southeastern tip of the Miura Peninsula around a spot called Kenzaki.

To get there, take the Keihin Kyuko Line as far as Miura Kaigan Station, and from bus stop No. 2 catch a bus for Kenzaki (which used to be known as Tsurugizaki, and sometimes still is).

Alighting from the bus, follow the road to the left through the fields and head toward the lighthouse, which will soon loom large before you. Originally built by an Englishman in 1871, but rebuilt in 1926 after being severely damaged in the Great Kanto Earthquake of 1923, the lighthouse stands 41 meters high and is the largest on the Miura Peninsula.

Walk down to the rocky shore below the lighthouse, and this is the starting point for a "seaside hiking course" which stretches all the way along the coast as far as the small island of Jogashima. It's rocky nearly all the way, but this poses few problems except where wet, so suitable footwear should be worn.

After a short walk by the sea and around a couple of small bays, the path again leads up through some fields and you eventually come to the entrance to Jiunji Temple, or Shirahama Bishamonten, one of the seven Miura Peninsula temples of good luck. The temple is said to have been founded in 1368, and for a long time has been a favorite among local fishermen seeking luck and large hauls.

The course then drops back down to the coast again, and the next stop is the Bishamonten cave, created by sea erosion and thought to have been used as a dwelling in the ancient Yayoi Period. Several items including primitive fishing equipment, shells and human bones have been excavated there.

The sea in the vicinity of the cave is relatively quiet, and this is probably a good point at which to break the journey for a picnic lunch before continuing along the route. You'll meet fishermen all along the way, but particularly popular points for anglers seem to be on the next stretch of the course, between Bishamon and Miyakawa bays. Surf fish, parrot fish, black porgy, sillaginoids and opaleye are what they catch.

For the hiker, Jogashima Island comes into view from Miyakawa Bay and the journey is almost over. Pass under Jogashima Ohashi Bridge and keep on for about another 10 minutes until you come to a bus stop. There you can catch a bus to Misakiguchi on the Keihin Kyuko Line.

Course: Shinagawa to Miura Kaigan by Keihin Kyuko Line (just over 60 minutes by special express); bus to Kenzaki (15 minutes); walk to lighthouse (15 minutes); walk to Jiunji Temple (about 60 minutes); to cave (30 minutes); to Miyakawa Bay (25 minutes); to Jogashima Ohashi Bridge (45 minutes); bus to Misakiguchi Station (30 minutes).

The Biggest Buddha of All
鋸山

MOST people readily associate Kamakura and Nara with their Great Buddha statues, so it might come as a surprise to learn that there are actually two other *daibutsus* in the Kanto area, and that one of them is in fact the largest in Japan.

While the sitting height of the Kamakura Buddha is 11.36 meters and that of the Nara Buddha 16.2 meters, the Great Buddha of Nihonji Temple in Chiba Prefecture measures 21 meters. This Buddha is made of concrete and was completed in 1969 after four years of work. What it lacks in antiquity it certainly makes up for in height, the whole structure reaching higher than 31 meters.

The Chiba Daibutsu enjoys a splendid location on the side of Mount Nokogiri, with Tokyo Bay, the Miura Peninsula and sometimes Mount Fuji visible in the distance. It is easily reached from Hama Kanaya Station on the JNR Uchibo Line (just over 90 minutes by special express from Tokyo Station), or by ferry across Tokyo Bay from Kurihama (35 minutes and ¥480 per adult one way).

Those who arrive by ferry have a particularly good view of the 329-meter mountain, and the reason for its name is clear — the jagged and serrated rocks really resembling a saw, or *nokogiri.*

From the port, turn right onto National Highway 127 and walk past the small road leading left to the station until you reach a large signpost indicating the entrance to the ropeway. This takes you up the mountain in four minutes. From the observation platform there you'll see the sea in front of you, and behind you a car park and the gateway to the hiking course.

The ¥300 entrance ticket includes a handy pictorial map, so it's pretty difficult to lose your way. Most people head first for the large Goddess of Mercy statue carved into a steep cliff and finished in 1966 after six years' work. Above this is another observation platform and a spot called Jigoku Nozoki, or Glimpse of Hell, from where it is possible to look down directly over the perpendicular cliff created by quarry work in the past.

From there follow the path down and branch off right along a course which leads past clusters of small Buddhist statues, about 1,300 of which remain from a total of 1,553 carved out of stone toward the end of the 18th century. Unfortunately, many have by now lost their heads, but nonetheless several have amusing expressions typical of such statues and they act as a fine curtain-raiser for the larger image below.

Where the path forks, keep heading downward until you reach a wider roadway. Go left to reach the Great Buddha, located in a large Daibutsu Hiroba square and modeled after another statue said to have existed on the site at some time in the past. This is a good spot for a picnic snack, with drinks on sale from vending machines and shaded benches looking out over the sea.

The path going down from the entrance to the square leads to Nihonji Temple, dating from 725 and once a huge place, although now just a handful of buildings remain. Follow the path down past a small pond and through the temple's *niomon* gate and eventually, crossing the railway line and highway on the way, you come out at the beach near Hota Station, one stop along from Hama Kanaya. *Tokkyu* trains don't stop there, but buses go to Hama Kanaya and to the ferry. Total hiking time is about 80 minutes, excluding rests and diversions.

For those wishing to extend their trip, there are several *minshuku* and *ryokan* inns in the Hama Kanaya area, and also along the sea front at Katsuyama, next stop along from Hota.

The other "unknown" *daibutsu* in the Kanto area, by the way, is to be found near Shimo Akatsuka Station on the Tobu Tojo Line from Ikebukuro. It was constructed in 1977 and has a sitting height of 8 meters.

The Great Buddha of Nihonji Temple (top left). Hoping for good luck (top right), and a cluster of small statues marking the walking course.

From Bridge to Bridge

養老渓谷

IF you like bridges, a good place to visit is Yoro Keikoku in Chiba Prefecture, for the riverside hiking course around this picturesque gorge involves crossing over seven bridges of varying shapes and sizes, and affords views of several more.

The course starts at Yoro Keikoku Station on the Kominato Line. Despite lying in the heart of the Boso Peninsula, Yoro Keikoku is easily reached from Tokyo. Take the JNR Sobu Main Line express from Tokyo Station as far as Goi Station, and change for the Kominato Line train which reaches Yoro Keikoku in about an hour.

From the station exit, take the path to the right, cross the tracks and follow the asphalt road right. After a short walk this brings you to the first bridge, Hoei Bashi, and your first sight of the gorge.

Beyond the red iron Hoei Bashi you will pass a museum village of folk houses and implements. Where the road forks, go left, and a short while later you'll come to a narrow road leading down to the left and around to bridge No. 2, a white suspension bridge spanning the Yoro River.

Cross over, turn left and you come out at a main road lined with inns. Turn right, and soon a red suspension bridge comes into view. This is Kannon Bashi, and the steps on the far side take visitors through a tunnel in the cliff to the Shusse Kannon Temple. A rather nondescript place, this, but worth a detour if you're seeking promotion at work, as that is what it's dedicated to.

Recross Kannon Bashi and walk down to the river where a large white cliff sets the scene for the next bridge, which consists simply of wooden planks. Once safely over, follow the path to the left round the bend in the river and you reach a bridge of concrete stepping stones, one of two on the course following one after the other. In between you'll see two perpendicular cliff faces with the Kaburai River running between them and into the Yoro River. These cliffs once formed the walls of a tunnel called the Kobundo which was the talking point of the region until a typhoon destroyed the roof.

The Kobundo tunnel minus its roof (left), and stepping stones across the Yoro River.

Turn left after picking your way over the second set of stepping stones and carry on for about 100 meters until you come to Kyoei Bashi. Don't cross right over, but use it as a platform to look back over the gorge before following the road away to the right.

This pleasant country stroll ends in a series of short tunnels. After the last of these, walk on a little way and go right where the road forks. This leads to a bridge across the Kaburai River, thence to the Okuyoro Bungalow Village, where, if you wish, you can rent a hut for the night.

Beyond the village, the path climbs sharply. Turn right when you come to a main road, and you can be back at Yoro Keikoku Station in about 20 minutes after crossing over Hoei Bashi once more. Overall hiking time is about 2 hours 20 minutes.

If you're not yet ready to return to Tokyo, the seaside resorts of Onjuku and Katsuura are not far away. Take the train from Yoro Keikoku Station to Kazusa Nakano, the next and last station on the Kominato Line, and then change to the JNR Kihara Line for Ohara on the Pacific Coast. From there, trains run to Onjuku and Katsuura.

Where Toads Are Kings

筑波

THE toad isn't everybody's favorite animal, but there's no denying the popularity of Toad Rock on Mount Tsukuba in Ibaraki Prefecture. Hikers who reach the summit head straight for the toad-shaped boulder, and many amuse themselves by throwing stones into its open mouth.

Consequently, the toad has become something of a symbol of Mount Tsukuba, and the many souvenir shops and stalls at its foot sell everything from toad cookies and toad oil ointment for the skin to toads themselves.

Although the Gama Ishi or Toad Rock is a special delight, it's just one of many fascinating rock shapes which make hiking on Mount Tsukuba a constant source of interest. Others of note include the Great Bear Rock, the Mother's Womb Rock, Risshin Seki, or the Rock of Advancement (a place of pilgrimage for students facing examinations), and the Benkei Nana Modori.

The latter consists of a torii-shaped formation with the top rock, the "roof" of the tunnel, looking as if it will fall in at any time. The rock's name comes from the legend that even the fearless and mighty Benkei hesitated seven times before finally passing through it.

Mount Tsukuba (the name derives from a word in the Ainu language meaning "towering head") is reached by taking the JNR Joban Line from Ueno Station as far as Tsuchiura, then changing to the local one-carriage Tsukuba Line of the Kanto Railway. A bus for Tsukuba Shrine, at the foot of the mountain, leaves from right in front of Tsukuba Station.

From the bus stop, it's a short walk up to the shrine's main hall. Take the path going off to the left and you will come to the cable car station. A trip to the top costs ¥360.

To say the "top" of the mountain is somewhat misleading, as Mount Tsukuba has two summits, on each of which stands an inner sanctuary of the main Tsukuba Shrine below. To the left of the cable car terminus rises the Nantai (Male) peak (870 meters high), with a short nature trail and a meteorological station, while to the right is the Nyotai (Female) peak, a little taller at 876 meters.

It's usual to climb the male peak first, then walk back past the cable car and up the female peak, which is a rocky summit offering the best views.

On the way up the female peak you'll see the Gama Ishi on the left, while the route down passes most of the other rocks. It takes about 30 minutes to reach the Benkei Nana Modori tunnel, and a short way beyond this, at a resting place, the path divides into two; go left for Tsukuba Shrine.

The descent, although steep, shouldn't pose too many problems, except for a couple of rocky and twisting sections where iron chains are provided to help hikers on their way.

Course: Ueno to Tsuchiura by the JNR Joban Line (50 minutes); Tsuchiura to Tsukuba by the Tsukuba Line (35 minutes); Tsukuba Station to Tsukuba Shrine by bus (15 minutes); cable car (8 minutes); hike up male peak (40 minutes); hike up female peak (20 minutes); down to Benkei Nana Modori rock (30 minutes); down to Tsukuba Shrine (50 minutes); back to Tsukuba Station by bus (15 minutes).

For those going by car, Tsutsujigaoka has a car park, and a ropeway carries visitors up from there to close by the female peak. The Tsukuba Gama Matsuri (Toad Festival) is held on Aug. 1-2 each year.

Rock shapes on Mount Tsukuba (left) and Tsukuba Shrine.

41

Kannon, Darumas and a Nature Trail

高崎

TAKASAKI in Gunma Prefecture is famous for two things: its giant statue of Kannon, the goddess of mercy, and its Daruma Temple. The two are some distance apart, but can be seen comfortably in a day thanks to the 8-km Takasaki Shizen Hodo (nature trail) hiking course.

The town can be reached in 76 minutes from Ueno Station by special express on the JNR Takasaki Line. This makes the fare a little expensive at ¥2,600, but it beats the local train by about 45 minutes. The station is also on the JNR Joetsu Shinkansen Line.

There are a number of bus stops outside Takasaki Station. The Joshin bus for Kannon-yama leaves from stop No. 2 and reaches its destination in about 15 minutes, via Dokutsu (Cave) Kannon and Kappapia amusement ground. These can be included in your itinerary if you decide to visit only the Kannon statue and park and leave the Daruma Temple for another day.

The Takasaki Kannon statue, or Byakui Daikannon as it's also called, is visible from the bus terminus, so you won't have any trouble finding it. Built in 1936, the statue stands 42 meters high. Entrance to the interior costs ¥200, and nine flights of stairs lead up to the top. On the way you pass by 20 statues of Buddhist figures such as Kobo Daishi, Nichiren and Kishi-bojin.

To reach the Shizen Hodo hiking course, take the path leading off behind the Kannon statue. Turn left when you come to a road, and you'll see the entrance to the course just ahead of you. Once under way there's no getting lost as the route is well signposted. After the first stretch of hill walking, you come to another road. Turn right there, and follow it — and the signs — for several minutes until you find yourself back on the mountain path. The area around the Kannon statue is also designated as a wild bird preservation district, so keep eyes and ears open.

Near the end of the mountain path, there is a small cave called the Daikoku Hole, possibly used as a grave in centuries gone by but also apparently a local place of worship. It is signposted, but lies just off the main path, so be careful not to miss it.

Soon you emerge at a road again and the markers direct you to turn left. Keep going, and you'll come upon some good views of the Takasaki Kannon on one side and Mount Asama (2,542 meters) and Mount Haruna (1,391 meters) on the other.

All told, it takes about two hours to complete the course to Shorinzan Daruma Temple. There is very little uphill walking involved.

The temple itself consists of several buildings, including the main hall and the Senshintei, which for a time was the home of Bruno Taut, the German architect who lived in Takasaki from 1934 to 1936. The main focus of interest, however, is the Takasaki daruma doll, symbol of good luck and perseverance.

The Daruma Temple is a pleasant place at any time, but you might want to note in your diary that its daruma fair takes place on January 6 and 7 every year.

From the temple, it's a 10-minute walk to National Route 18 — crossing the Usui River on the way — and the Hachiman Daimon bus stop for buses back to Takasaki Station. If you have time, however, try walking a couple of stops in the direction of Takasaki, and you'll pass several houses where you can see the dolls being made.

And to round off your day trip, buy a *daruma ekiben,* or lunch box, at Takasaki Station for the train journey home. It's a tasty meal contained in a plastic daruma which afterward can be used as a piggy bank.

Fairs

A Fair With a Shitamachi Flavor

門前仲町

GIVEN the ease with which Buddhism and Shintoism co-exist in Japanese life, it is not at all surprising to find a temple and shrine coming together three times a month to host a local *ennichi* market.

The place to go is Monzennakacho in Tokyo's Koto Ward, a downtown area which still retains the spirit of its *shitamachi* past, despite being destroyed twice this century by earthquake and war, and even though its inhabitants must nowadays live in the shadow of Highway No. 9.

The temple in question is the Fukagawa Fudo, a branch temple of Narita Fudo in Chiba first built in 1703, while the shrine is the neighboring Tomioka Hachimangu, originally constructed in 1627 and certainly no stranger to festivals. Its annual Fukagawa *matsuri* held every August is particularly spectacular once every three years (1983, 1986 and so on).

For the local fair, which is held on the 1st, 15th and 28th of each month, take the east exit of Monzennakacho Station on the Tozai subway line. This brings you out onto Eitai-dori avenue, and the market stalls which line the pavement are already beckoning as you emerge.

Turn right out of the station and then right again, and a narrow road leads a few hundred meters up to Fukagawa Fudo, a place teeming with pigeons and people. At the entrance a young man works busily on some earpicks, one of the many interesting stalls which also sell *geta* clogs, *senbei* biscuits, pipes, tea, socks, various kinds of seafood and the biggest lumps of chocolate the author has ever seen.

Back to Eitai-dori, and stalls displaying household goods and numerous snacks continue in the direction of Eitai Bridge, while to the left, in the direction of Kiba, the pavement is lined with flowers and plants for a considerable distance.

Nearby is the torii of Tomioka Hachimangu, guarded by a large and impressive stone lantern. The traditions of the area are remembered in the grounds of this shrine through several stone monuments, one of them being the Yokozuna Rikishi monument weighing, appropriately enough, 24 tons. Sumo wrestling was held in the precincts of the shrine before bouts were moved to Ryogoku in 1791.

There are also monuments to *kaku-nori,* or log-rolling, and *chikara-mochi* (weightlifting). These were skills developed by lumberyard workers and raftsmen some 300 years ago when Kiba was a major center for lumber merchants and warehouses. They are now held as events in the Grand Tokyo Festival which takes place annually at the beginning of October.

The Tomioka Hachimangu-Fukagawa Fudo local fair is held from about 10 a.m. to 6 p.m. although stalls stay out until about 9 p.m. in the summer months. Monzennakacho is often overlooked as a "leisure" spot, but the temple and shrine and surrounding *shitamachi* area are well worth a visit, especially on fair day.

In Search of Tora-san's Roots

柴又

PICTURE a quiet-flowing river flanked by green and gently sloping embankments. No cows or sheep are in sight, but here and there families enjoy a picnic, fishermen snooze by their rods in the afternoon sun and in the distance some figures play out a game of golf. Completing this tranquil scene, a wooden ferry plies its way between the banks, punted by an experienced and affable boatman.

The setting is the Edogawa River in northeastern Tokyo, and the ferry the only one of its kind still remaining in the capital. From the early Edo Period — from 1631, to be precise — it was used to carry farmers over the 140-meter stretch of water separating Chiba Prefecture from Tokyo's Shibamata, but now it's tourists who pack themselves into the narrow vessel for the five-minute trip.

The Yagiri ferry can take over 20 people at a time and costs ¥100 for adults and ¥50 for children. For most of the year it operates only on Saturdays, Sundays and holidays, but from March until around the end of June it runs every day from morning until evening, weather permitting.

This is to cater to the tourists who are visiting the area in increasing numbers, attracted by the unique river crossing and by Shibamata's appeal as the setting of the popular "Tora-san" series of films. As the *shitamachi* hero always says proudly of himself, "Born and bred in Katsushika, Shibamata . . ."

From Shibamata Station on the Keisei Line from Ueno (change onto the branch line for Kanamachi at Takasago and Shibamata is the next stop), the road leading straight ahead for some 200 meters is lined with old-fashioned stores selling the local green *kusa* dumplings, *senbei* biscuits, *daruma* dolls, candies and various other souvenirs such as the popular *hajiki-saru* (springing monkeys). Midway along on the right is "Toraya," the shop used in the movies.

At the end of the road is the "Tora-san temple," Shibamata Taishakuten, a Nichiren temple founded in 1629. The story goes that

48

Guiding the Yagiri ferry across the Edogawa.

the temple's image of Buddha at some time disappeared, only to reappear again miraculously during reconstruction work in 1779, a phenomenon which inevitably caught the imagination of people at the time.

Pilgrims began to flock to the temple from all parts of Edo, and a local fair was started. The fair is held about once every two months on the day of the sexagenary cycle on which the image made its reappearance. Check local newspapers for dates. Stalls are set up along the street leading from the station and in the temple precincts, and remain open throughout the day.

Taishakuten is also famous for its wood carvings of scenes from the Lotus Sutra, completed during the 1920s and early 1930s.

The Yagiri ferry is just behind the temple. Turn left in front of the temple gate, then right, and walk down to the river. After the trip, follow the flow of the river and eventually you will come to a bridge carrying the JNR Sobu Line, with Ichikawa Station on one side and Koiwa on the other.

Rubbing Away the Pain

巣鴨

IF anyone thinks traditional beliefs are disappearing in modern-day Japan, they should try visiting Togenuki-Jizo in Tokyo's Sugamo district.

In the narrow precincts of the temple they will find a long line of people, young and old, waiting their turn to pour water over a small stone Jizo statue. They then proceed to rub this Migawari-Jizo vigorously with a scrubbing brush on the areas where their own body hurts — head, shoulders, back or wherever they happen to be suffering.

Scrubbing the germs away. . .

The faithful believe that by doing this their aches and pains will be relieved, and so strong is the belief that the temple is always crowded and the poor statue's face has been well and truly worn away.

As well as being congested, Koganji, as the temple is otherwise called, is also a smokey place. Just inside the entrance stands a large urn into which visitors throw incense sticks sold at various spots in the area. It is thought that if the billowing smoke is rubbed into the body, pain will be relieved.

It all started back in 1715 when a young woman swallowed a needle which she had been holding in her mouth. After other attempts to extract it had failed, she took a paper image of the Jizo of the temple, which at that time was located in Ueno, and swallowed it with a cup of water — with the result that she was safely relieved of the needle. From that time on, Koganji Temple became better known as Togenuki-Jizo.

The temple, first built in 1598, was moved from Ueno's Byobuzaka to Sugamo in 1891. Until then the area had lacked sparkle, but with the coming of the popular temple, and the opening of Sugamo Station in 1903, it was transformed into the bustling district it is today.

So if you have any illnesses worrying you, or if you just want to see the tradition being carried on, visit Togenuki-Jizo. The most convenient approach is from JNR Sugamo Station on the Yamanote Line, from where Jizo-dori shopping street is a short walk to the north.

Alternatively, an interesting way to arrive is by Tokyo's last remaining streetcar, the Arakawa Line running between Waseda and Minowa. Get off at Koshinzuka Station, and head along Jizo-dori shopping street toward Sugamo. If you go on the 4th, 14th or 24th of the month, you'll notice the special atmosphere because it's local fair day, and you'll soon come across stalls selling antiques, clothing, candies and food.

Togenuki-Jizo *ennichi* is one of the biggest fairs in Tokyo, and excels itself on the 24th of January, May and September respectively. The temple is to be found about three-quarters of the way along the street toward Sugamo Station on the lefthand side.

Remembering the 47 Ronin

泉岳寺

IF you want to see the graves of the 47 *ronin* at Sengakuji Temple in Tokyo's Minato Ward, try and avoid going on December 14, the anniversary of their attack on the home of Lord Kira. On this day the temple holds a commemorative festival when the last resting place of the famous 47 disappears in a thick cloud of smoke rising from the bundles of incense sticks proffered by people coming to pay their respects.

In 1701, Naganori Asano, the lord of Ako Castle in the present Hyogo Prefecture, drew his sword in Edo Castle after being insulted by Yoshinaka Kira, the official overseer of ceremonies and by all accounts a "man of mean intent." For this crime, Asano was forced to commit suicide, and the injustice of his fate so riled his retainers that they pledged to revenge their master's death.

First of all they renounced their allegiance to the dead lord in order not to implicate his family and became ronin, or masterless samurai. Then, on the night of December 14 the following year, they broke through the guard at Kira's residence near Ryogoku Bridge, hunted out their enemy and killed him.

After offering Kira's head to their lord's grave, the ronin gave themselves up to the authorities and, upon being ordered to do so, took their own lives on February 4, 1703. They were buried by the grave of Lord Asano at Sengakuji Temple, and to this day are the focus of much attention, especially on the anniversary of their deed. While the temple grounds are crowded with stalls selling all kinds of festival items, including sweet sake to repel the winter cold, a long queue forms on the steps leading up to the graves. Many emerge from the small cemetery wiping tears from their eyes, though whether in remembrance of the heroic deed of the ronin or because of the cloying incense, it's hard to say.

This Gishi-sai festival continues throughout the day, but climaxes in the evening when a costume parade re-enacting the vendetta takes place. The procession starts near Ryogoku Bridge and after a reception in Matsuzakacho Park, takes the subway to Sengakuji where a service is held in the temple's main hall, usually at about 7:30 p.m.

Sengakuji Temple is a short walk from the station of the same name on the Toei Asakusa subway line. It was originally built in 1612 near Edo Castle on the orders of Tokugawa Ieyasu, and was later rebuilt at its present site in Takanawa after being completely destroyed by a fire.

Just in front of the main gate is a statue of Oishi Yoshio, the leader of the 47 ronin, and beyond are the main hall, which dates from the mid-19th century, a bell tower, and the Gishikan Museum containing items related to the famous event and models of all the characters involved. Entrance is ¥200. The graves are on a small hill behind this museum and at the foot of the steps leading up to them is the Kubiarai Ido well, where Kira's head was washed before being presented to the grave of Lord Asano.

If you happen to be in Hyogo Prefecture on this date, then the place to head for is Ako City, where several historical sites associated with the loyal retainers can be seen and where a similar Gishi-sai festival is held at the Oishi Shrine, dedicated to the leader of the ronin.

Sengakuji Temple in
Minato Ward.

The Largest Plant Fair in Kanto

池上本門寺

IKEGAMI Honmonji Temple barely has time to recover from an invasion of cherry-blossom viewers before it must prepare for another onslaught by flower-lovers, this time for the annual plant fair which lasts from April 25 until May 5.

The fair, claimed to be the largest plant market in Kanto, is held in the spacious precincts of the temple, which is a short walk to the north from Ikegami Station on the Tokyu Ikegami Line running between Gotanda and Kamata. Follow the road leading directly away from the station exit (Honmonji-dori), turn right where it ends and then immediately left. Cross the small river by way of Ryozenbashi Bridge, and facing you are the 96 stone steps which lead up into the temple grounds.

Over 70 traders take part in the fair every year, turning the temple into a botanical garden as they sell varieties of cactus, azalea and other plants at very reasonable prices. Both sellers and buyers gather from all over the Kanto region for this once-a-year attraction.

If you can take your eyes off the flowers and plants for a while, there is also a lot to see of Honmonji itself. The temple has a history going back to 1276 when it was built by Ikegami Munenaka, a local lord who was a devoted follower of Nichiren. It was at Ikegami Munenaka's residence, in fact, that Nichiren passed away on Oct. 13, 1282, and a large *oeshiki* festival is held at the temple between October 11 and 13 marking the anniversary of his death.

The temple was severely damaged by the air raids of 1945, everything disappearing except the five-story pagoda to the right of the main hall, and the *kyozo*, or sutra house, and *hoto* tower, both to its left. The 29-meter pagoda was built in 1607, a contribution of the second shogun, Tokugawa Hidetada, while the sutra house was built in 1784 and has inside it the Buddhist scriptures. The *hoto* tower was built in 1830 and stands on the site where Nichiren was cremated.

Other buildings are therefore of relatively recent construction, the

Before the plants arrive —
open space at Ikegami
Honmonji Temple.

main hall with its image of Nichiren having been completed in 1964
and the temple gate with its guardian gods in 1977. On the pagoda
side of the temple there is a large cemetery and Ikegami Honmonji
Park, which has a small fishing pond. The 96 steps, by the way, were
laid at the beginning of the 17th century and represent the number of
scriptures found in the *hoto* tower.

But back to plants and plant fairs. As well as the Ikegami Honmonji
market, others worth noting are:

Konpira-san plant fair: Every month on the 25th, along the
road leading from Toranomon Crossing to Shinbashi Station. From
Toranomon Subway Station.

Yurakucho-Otemachi flower fair: Every month on the 7th and
8th except when these days fall on a weekend. By North Chuo Kinko
Bldg. (from Yurakucho Station) and Nokyo Bldg. (from Shinbashi
Station). Good for a lunch-hour stroll!

O-Fuji-san plant fair: May 31-June 1 and June 30-July 1, on the
streets around Sengen Shrine in Asakusa from Asakusa Subway
Station (Asakusa 5-chome). This fair dates from the mid-Meiji
Period.

Zenyoji rose and azalea fair: At Zenyoji Temple in Higashi
Koiwa, Edogawa Ward, a 20-minute walk from Koiwa Station on
the JNR Sobu Line. Usually held for five days around the last weekend
in May.

The Roots of
Sweet Potatoes

目黒不動

IF it hadn't been for Tokugawa Iemitsu's falcon, Meguro Fudo probably wouldn't be the popular temple it is today. Ryusenji, as the temple is more formally known, was originally founded in the year 808 by the priest Jikaku Daishi, but eight centuries were to pass before it made a name for itself.

The story goes that the third shogun's falcon escaped and only returned after special prayers were said by a priest at the temple. Overjoyed, Iemitsu gave orders for the building of a main hall, which was erected in 1634. His patronage meant that Meguro Fudo became a bustling place in the Edo Period, and reminders of that past are still to be seen on the 28th of each month, when the temple holds its *ennichi* fair.

The temple buildings were destroyed in the war and the *niomon* gate, bell tower and main hall later rebuilt, but what it lacks in historical authenticity, Meguro Fudo makes up for in grandeur.

Beyond the gate, with its fierce-looking Deva King statues warding off evil spirits, the temple grounds stretch out to left and right. Directly ahead is a flight of steps leading to the summit of a hill on which is perched the main hall. At the foot of these steps is a waterfall, said to have been created when Jikaku Daishi tossed down his iron club and water spouted forth.

On the summit of the hill is the *hondo* hall, now a shining and colorful ferro-concrete structure. It is in this area, under the fine gingko and other trees, as well as at the foot of the hill and around the entrance gate, that stalls congregate on fair day.

Meguro Fudo also has associations with sweet potatoes. The narrow road away to the right of the main hall leads to the grave of Aoki Konyo (1698-1769), a scholar of Dutch learning who wrote on sweet potato cultivation and advocated sweet potatoes as an answer to famine during the Edo Period. Aoki ("Kansho sensei") spend his later years in the Meguro district, and every October 28 sees not only a local temple fair, but a special sweet potato festival as well.

A short walk beyond the main hall is Fudo Park, worth visiting for its small botanical garden.

Since 1978, local markets have also been held at Meguro Fudo on the 8th and 18th of each month, but these are small affairs and the 28th remains the best day on which to drop by.

The temple is a 10-minute walk from Fudomae Station on the Tokyu Mekama Line. When approaching from Meguro, leave Fudomae Station, cross the railway line and follow the narrow winding road until you come to a junction. Cross the main road there, and walk left until you reach a gas station. Turn right beyond there, and the road leads to the temple gate. Alternatively, Tokyu bus No. 72 running between JNR Shibuya and Gotanda stations stops in front of the temple.

A Western-Style Gateway in Koenji

妙法寺

WHAT do Nicolai Cathedral in Tokyo's Chiyoda Ward, the old Ueno Museum (predecessor of the Tokyo National Museum), the original Marunouchi business district and Myohoji Temple in Suginami Ward all have in common?

The answer is that they were all influenced by the design skills of Josiah Conder (1852-1920), an Englishman who came to Japan in 1877 and played a significant role in shaping Japan's Meiji-Period architecture. Indeed, as a professor at Tokyo Imperial University, Conder helped educate a new generation of Japanese architects in Western-style construction and design.

The cathedral and museum were two of his most representative works, while he started, and later supervised, construction of the Marunouchi district, apparently in imitation of London's Lombard Street.

His contribution to the temple was small but lasting — a five-meter-high iron gate which he built in 1878 and which still stands today at the entrance to the temple precincts. It is now designated as an Important Cultural Asset. In its design Conder seems to have succeeded in blending Western and Oriental styles to give this noted institution of the Nichiren Sect an unusual but by no means incongruous gateway.

Details of the origins of Myohoji Temple itself are unclear, but its highly ornate Soshido hall contains a wooden image of Nichiren, the founder of the sect, said to have been carved by his disciple Nichiro (1243-1320) when Nichiren was 42 years of age. The temple was probably first built some time in the 17th century.

The temple is located in extensive grounds and includes the said Soshido hall, the main temple building, a study hall and the *romon,* another gateway. The statue of Nichiren was thought to charm away misfortune, and Myohoji became a popular place for worshippers in the Edo Period, to the extent that it was ranked along with Asakusa Kannon as a mecca for believers and day trippers.

It still is a popular place with young children darting about among the buildings and monuments and elderly persons enjoying a game of gateball (similar to croquet), and on the 13th and 23rd of each month it becomes even more crowded as dozens of stalls are set up on the approach road and inside the temple grounds.

As well as candy, *yakisoba,* corn, *takoyaki,* goldfish and balloons, several stalls sell antiques and old clothing. The fair lasts throughout the day until early evening.

Myohoji Temple is easily reached from Higashi-Koenji Station on the Marunouchi subway line. From the station, walk away from Nakano along Ome Kaido to the junction with the Kanjo 7-go expressway (*kan-nana*), turn left and walk until you reach the Myohoji crossing. Cross there, and the shopping street leads to the temple.

Alternatively, Myohoji can be reached by the "temple route." From the south exit of JNR Koenji Station on the Chuo Line, follow the road which branches off to the left, passes Hikawa Shrine and Koenji Central Park, and leads to Koenji Temple. There are about 30 temples on Koenji's south side, and with no really large buildings in the area, if you keep heading south, the temple roofs introduce themselves.

Turn right when you come to Ome Kaido, then left after walking as far as Shin-Koenji Station, from where Myohoji is a 10-minute walk to the southeast. Some of the temples are newly built but several are worth a visit — Koenji for its tea garden, Horinji for its huge wooden *shamoji* ladle, Choryuji for its Tofu-Jizo statue, and, of course, Myohoji, which also holds a large festival every year on October 12-13.

A Blessing for Your Car

西新井大師

IT'S not at all unusual to find rows of cars lined up facing the main hall of Nishiarai Daishi Temple in Tokyo's Adachi Ward. Although at first sight it might appear that worshippers have simply found a very convenient parking space, the vehicles are there for a special purpose.

Stay around, and eventually you will see drivers standing smartly in front of their possessions as a priest takes his position at a small podium before them. After a general prayer, the priest proceeds to each individual car and gives a blessing which, it is hoped, will guard them from road accidents — for Nishiarai Daishi is another temple dedicated to traffic safety.

The quaint ceremony is held half a dozen times a day, at the same time as cedar-stick burning rites are conducted inside the main hall to ward off evil spirits. People wishing to take part have to apply to the temple beforehand, but just watching is interesting, especially if you time your visit to coincide with the temple's *ennichi* fair on the 1st and 21st of every month.

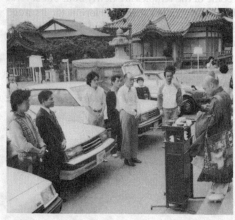

Cars — and drivers — receive a blessing.

The temple, properly called Sojiji, is near Daishimae Station on the branch line running from Tobu Isezaki Line's Nishiarai Station. It is particularly well-known for its peony garden, irises and a 700-year old wisteria tree as well as large aviaries inhabited by hens, pheasants, peacocks and other birds. There are also numerous statues dotted around the main hall, including the drenched Mizukake-Jizo, the Shio-Jizo covered in salt, a statue of the priest Kobo Daishi (774-835) to whom the temple is dedicated, and a cluster of small Buddhist images.

The temple is also traditionally thought to offer protection from fires, a belief stemming from the fact that several fires over the centuries since the temple's founding in the late 820s left the buildings in ruins but apparently failed to harm the temple's main image.

Fair days see the grounds filled with stalls selling candy, goldfish, clothing and so on. Daruma dolls, plants, vegetables and fruit are for sale along nearby streets.

Another large *daishi* temple in the Kanto area is Heigenji, popularly known as Kawasaki Daishi and said to have been founded in 1128 when a samurai named Hirama Kanenori scooped up a wooden statue of Kobo Daishi from the sea following a dream. Like Nishiarai Daishi, most of the temple has been rebuilt in recent years, and it also is located near a Daishimae Station on a branch line, in this case the line which runs from Keihin Kyuko Kawasaki Daishi Station. Alternatively, a bus may be taken to the temple from in front of JNR Kawasaki Station.

Kawasaki Daishi is renowned for the crowds it draws at New Year's, some rating it as Japan's No. 1 spot for *hatsumode* visits. Less overwhelming but still very popular are the temple's monthly ennichi fairs held on the 21st, with around 50 stalls offering all kinds of attractions, including darumas. As with the Nishiarai fair, Kawasaki Daishi's ennichi runs from about 9 a.m. until early evening.

A Monthly Bonanza in Chofu

布多天神

CHOFU to the west of Tokyo is famous for its airport, and for Jindaiji Temple and botanical gardens which are located a short bus ride from Chofu Station. Less well-known is Fuda Tenjin Shrine, just a five-minute walk from the station on the Keio Line.

On most days it is a quiet place, tucked away from the busy shopping area around the station, but on the 25th of each month it becomes the lively site of the Fuda Tenjin fair, a local market which before the war is said to have been on a par with the popular Setagaya *boro-ichi* with as many as 600 shops setting up their stalls there.

Fuda was the third post-town on the Koshu-Kaido highway during the Edo Period, and the history of the market goes back to those times. Although smaller in scale now, it is still held each month with a variety of stalls lining the approach road to the shrine.

The site becomes particularly crowded beyond the *torii* gate. The narrow pathway is lined on both sides by stalls offering *okonomiyaki* pancakes, chocolate bananas, candies and the chance to scoop yourself some goldfish. Children throng this area, trying their luck at winning extra toffee apples or "sauce *senbei*" from the friendly stallkeepers.

Behind these stalls to the right various plants are up for sale, while to the left a dozen or so "merchants" dispense with stalls and spread their wares out on the ground under the trees. This is the area where adult visitors congregate, hunting for bargains among the variety of goods offered.

"At ¥200 it's easier to buy it than listen to my explanation of what it is!" calls one man in a corner to a bemused customer inspecting one of the numerous odds and ends, the recognizable among which are old drums, clocks, recorders, lamps and shoes. Elsewhere, a gentleman offers tape recorders and radios, another deals in old books, stamps, records and the like, and another is surrounded by real antiques at quite expensive prices.

"There's only one shop in all Tokyo offering this cheaply, and that's me,'' shouts another man, indicating a toy robot-like figure from a famous TV cartoon program, while an old woman is almost hidden by the kimono materials she is selling. One round of the stalls is completely insufficient, second and third inspections revealing more and more surprises among the used bags, clothes, household goods and saws both old and new.

Fuda Tenjin Shrine was originally located near the Tama River, but as a result of flooding was moved to its present spot in 1477. In its grounds are a pair of lion-shaped guardian dogs (*komainu*), said to have been donated in 1796 by merchants hoping for business prosperity and the success of the fair.

To reach the shrine, take the north exit of Chofu Station and walk straight ahead to the Old Koshu-Kaido highway. Crossing this, take the narrow Tenjin-dori street which leads directly to the new Koshu-Kaido highway; cross this and you enter the approach road to the shrine. The fair is held from around mid-day until dark.

How to spend those last few yen . . .?

Scooping for goldfish.

Festivals and Facades in Fuchu

大国魂神社

WHEN asked what singles out Fuchu City in western Tokyo, many people will probably answer horse-racing, because of the large racecourse that is located there. In fact, the city has two other attractions for which it is well known (three, counting Japan's largest prison), one being its shrine and the other its remaining Meiji-Period tradesmen's houses.

There are several small temples and shrines in Fuchu, such as Shomyoji near the station, but the center of attention is Okunitama Shrine near the west exit of Fuchu Station on the Keio Line from Shinjuku, and reached along a road lined with giant *keyaki*, or zelkova trees.

One explanation has it that these trees were planted in 1614 on the orders of the first Tokugawa shogun, Ieyasu; it was under the patronage of the Tokugawa shogunate that the shrine buildings were reconstructed in the middle of the 17th century.

The shrine itself is said to date from 111, and was called Rokusho Shrine until 1871, when it was given its present name.

As well as the impressive approach road and shrine buildings, and the museum of local history in its grounds, Okunitama also has a full calendar of festivals and fairs. The main event at the shrine during the year is the Kurayami Darkness Festival, which takes place on May 5.

The history of this festival goes back almost to the time of the original founding of the shrine. It apparently came to be called the Kurayami Festival about 700 years ago, the name being connected with the fact that the festive *mikoshi* processions used to take place in the middle of the night. Nowadays, for reasons of public safety, the processions are held in the early evening.

On July 20 comes the shrine's Sumomo Plum Festival, and a Kuri Chestnut Festival is held on September 27 and 28 each year. Both of these festivals start about 10 a.m. and last all day. Okunitama Shrine is also well known for its Misoka Ichi fair held annually on New Year's Eve, from 10 a.m. until well into the night, with many stalls selling items related to the season's festivities.

While the keyaki road runs north to south through the city, the old Koshu-Kaido highway cuts across from east to west, passing in front of the shrine's torii archway. For a glimpse of Fuchu's past as a merchant town, turn left onto this highway as you leave the shrine and keep going until you reach the first main junction.

On one corner there is an old *soba* restaurant, and on another stands the site which the central government in the Edo Period used as a "bulletin board" for issuing public announcements. Fuchu at that time was an important post-town on the route to the capital.

Turning left at the junction, go past the city hall. On the right you'll see an old fishmonger's shop, and on the next corner a rice merchant's store. Follow the road to the left there, and you'll find yourself back in the grounds of Okunitama Shrine, with the main hall to the right and the local history museum to the left.

Okunitama Shrine

A Mini-Pilgrimage in Hino City

高幡不動

IF you don't have time to go down to Shikoku, then head for Hino City to the west of Tokyo. In the wooded hill behind Hino's Takahata Fudo Temple there is a hiking course marked by 88 small statues in miniature imitation of the 88 sacred places in Shikoku visited by followers of the priest Kobo Daishi. The Shikoku pilgrimage takes over a month to complete properly, but under an hour is needed at Takahata Fudo.

The starting point is just in front of the temple's pagoda, the path winding quickly away past statues marked one, two, three and so on up to an observation point on the hill, then back down to the 88th and final statue at the small Daishido temple building.

Takahata Fudo Temple itself, properly called Kingoji and one of the three famous Kanto Fudo temples (the others being Oyama in Kanagawa Prefecture and Narita-Shinshoji in Chiba), was originally founded around the beginning of the eighth century. It is now a striking mixture of old and new.

The 45-meter five-storied pagoda, looming up behind the old temple gate which greets visitors, is a new and sparkling structure copying early Heian-Period design. It was completed in 1979, and on the hill beyond is a shining new bell tower built to commemorate its erection. To the left of the temple entrance is a Kotsu Anzen Kigan hall, so don't be surprised if you see traffic police milling round the temple precincts because Takahata Fudo is dedicated to traffic safety.

There are over 20 structures of various kinds dotted around the temple grounds. The *niomon* gate was built in 1342 when the temple, which was originally located on the top of the hill, was rebuilt in its present, more sheltered location, after being brought down in a terrific gale in 1335. The building beyond the temple and guarded by a *sanmon* gate is the Dainichido hall, built in the mid-Edo Period with a Dainichi Buddha figure dating from the Heian Period and a famous Crying Dragon on the ceiling of the outer chamber. The echo of clapped hands is said to make the dragon appear to cry out, and a wish made at this time will come true.

There are also various monuments around the temple, and on the hill just behind the pagoda is a "Nose Well," this supposedly the spot where the nose of the Fudo deity landed when it was swept away in the 1335 gale.

Takahata Fudo Temple is very near the station of the same name on the Keio Line from Shinjuku. Altenatively, it can be reached by bus from Hino Station on the JNR Chuo Line (the bus stop is just behind the station). The pagoda can be clearly seen from the approaching train and from the exit to Takahata Fudo Station. A good day to go is the 28th of the month, when the temple holds its regular *ennichi* fair. Especially popular are Takahata *manju* and bamboo baskets which people come from afar to buy.

For those who like their day trips long and varied, Takahata Fudo is also a good starting point for visits to several other spots in the area, the most popular of which being Tama Zoo at Tama Dobutsuen Station on the Keio branch line from Takahata Fudo (open 9 a.m.-4:30 p.m., closed Mondays); Tama Tech amusement park, a five-minute bus ride from the zoo (open 9 a.m.-5 p.m. every day), and Mogusaen, a garden particularly famous for its plum blossoms. The latter is 10 minutes from Mogusaen Station on the Keio Line, one stop toward Shinjuku from Takahata Fudo. It is open from 9 a.m.-4 p.m. and closed on Wednesdays.

The Daishido, last stop on Takahata Fudo's pilgrimage course.

A Cartoon in Stone in Little Edo

川越

THEY don't tell any particular story, but the Five Hundred Rakan in Kawagoe could well be called a cartoon in stone. Numbering 540 statues altogether, they depict priests who have succeeded in renouncing the material world and attaining enlightenment.

It took nearly 50 years to complete the sculptures after they were started in 1782 by a Kawagoe priest called Shijo, and the result is a wonderful collection of human expressions and poses, some amused, some sad, some upright — and several reclining.

Look for the pair who are holding a whispered conversation, or the priest who seems to be weeping. There's one boiling water on a stove, another engrossed in reading, and a third who sports a pair of spectacles. No two sculptures are the same.

The Five Hundred Rakan are located in a corner of Kitain Temple in Kawagoe, Saitama Prefecture, a 10-minute walk from Hon-Kawagoe Station on the Seibu Shinjuku Line, or from Kawagoe Station on the Tobu Tojo Line.

The temple, founded in the year 830 by the priest Jikaku Daishi, includes several buildings transferred to the site from Edo Castle by the third Tokugawa shogun, Iemitsu (1604-1651), after a fire destroyed the original buildings in 1638.

Only the temple gate remained after the fire, and Iemitsu ordered an annex at Edo Castle to be moved there. This included a reception hall and study and, it is said, the room in which Iemitsu was born. Other buildings were put up on the spot, including the bell tower and the Tahoto tower, the Jiedo and Jigendo halls, and the Toshogu and Hie shrines, which since the Meiji Restoration have been under separate jurisdiction.

Toshogu Shrine, just south of Kitain, is one of three well-known shrines of the same name, the others being on Mount Kunozan in Shizuoka and in Nikko. The Kawagoe Toshogu Shrine was erected after the remains of Tokugawa Ieyasu (1542-1616) were brought

Sharing a secret.

there in 1617 on their way from Kunozan, where he died, to Nikko.

Kitain Temple is a popular place, and the Five Hundred Rakan a "must" for camera enthusiasts. An admission ticket costs ¥200 and covers the annex building, the main temple hall, and the statues, which you will find behind the refreshment booths in the temple grounds.

In the annex is a splendid six-fold screen painting featuring illustrations of 25 artisans of the early 17th century.

The temple is the site of a daruma fair on January 3 and February 3 every year, and a four-day plant market held in mid-May and September. A short walk away is Kawagoe Fudo Temple where Tokyo Flea Market ("Nomi no Ichi") members and locals sell their antique wares on the 28th of every month. Kawagoe Festival is held annually between October 14 and 15.

An early start is advisable for anyone wishing to "do" Kawagoe in a day, for "Little Edo," as the town is often called, has much to offer. As well as Kitain and its neighboring temples and shrines, a walking tour should take in the site of the castle, the Edo-Period Osawa House and other old buildings near it, and the clock tower, first built in 1653 and still the symbol of the town today.

Pottery, Pottery Everywhere

益子

WHEN visiting Mashiko, it's a good idea to take along a large, empty bag, especially if you make the trip during Golden Week at the beginning of May or at the start of November, the two times in the year when this pottery town in Tochigi Prefecture holds its ceramics fair.

The temptation to stock up with all the necessary items for kitchen and living room in one sweep is great, particularly at fair time when prices are cheap. One-hundred yen corners offer coffee mugs and tea cups, rice bowls and plates, while sets of dishes, cups and saucers, and *tokkuri* for Japanese sake sell for between ¥1,200 and ¥1,500.

It's no wonder that the two women sitting opposite on the train going home could be seen searching through their many packages, trying to remember everything they had bought.

If it seems too good to be true, a word of warning is perhaps in order. Some of the bargains on sale at the fair might have cracks or chips, either original defects or the result of being handled by too many prospective buyers, so it is wise to be extra careful when purchasing on the cheap.

The ceramics fair, which started in 1968, certainly adds to the fun of visiting Mashiko, although it's worth arriving early to avoid the crowds and to allow yourself time to see the rest of the town as well.

Mashiko is on the local JNR Moka Line running from Oyama, but there are few trains, so it's better to take the JNR Tohoku Main Line from Ueno as far as Utsunomiya, and from there catch a Toya bus to Mashiko, saving the Moka Line for the journey home in the evening.

Take the road leading straight ahead from Utsunomiya Station, and the bus stop is just to the left at the first set of traffic lights. There are about two buses an hour.

Excavations have shown that pottery was an important activity in the area in the distant past, but the modern history of Mashiko-ware started in the 1850s, influenced by the ceramics of nearby Kasama. Then, in 1924, the famous potter Shoji Hamada set up a kiln in the town, and the area's fortunes began to blossom. The streets of Mashiko are now lined with shops making and selling local pottery and folkcraft goods.

The spring and autumn fairs are held in the square of the Kyohan Center, about 1 km from the station. On the righthand side of the road just before you reach the center is one of the latest additions to Mashiko's attractions, an outdoor pottery kiln museum. Entrance is ¥500, in return for which the owner, Yoshio Nakamura, and his wife give a guided tour with explanations (in Japanese) of the process of preparing clay and of the various kilns on display, ranging from an ancient earthen kiln to a *nobori-kama* climbing kiln and a modern kiln operated by computer. There are also displays of *haniwa* clay images made by Nakamura, and of Mashiko-ware ceramics.

Mashiko has more than just pottery to offer. From the museum, walk in the direction of the station, and at the first main junction you'll see a sign pointing left toward Saimyoji Temple. It's a 30-minute walk through quiet countryside, and well worth it to see the temple with its three-storied pagoda, and the thatched-roofed gateway and bell-tower which lend Saimyoji its rustic appearance.

From there it is possible to follow a 60-minute hiking course to Mashiko's Togei no Mori (Ceramics Wood) on the eastern side of the town, or return along the same road back to the station. From Mashiko it takes 70 minutes by the Moka Line to Oyama (you may have to change at Shimodate), and then 77 minutes back to Ueno by the JNR Tohoku Main Line.

Bargains Galore for Early Risers

朝市

A T one stage it looked as if the neighborhood store was fighting a losing battle in the face of competition from big chain supermarkets springing up everywhere.

However, local shopkeepers have been banding together and hitting back with a vengeance through their early-morning markets. *Asa-ichi* have a long tradition going back 400 years in the countryside and in fishing villages, famous ones being held in Takayama in Gifu, Wajima in Ishikawa and Katsuura in Chiba Prefecture.

In Tokyo, the morning market is a new phenomenon, but the number to have started up in recent years constitutes a veritable boom. The stores along a particular shopping street get together and on one or two Sundays each month set up stalls and turn their street into an open-air market.

The Tokyo asa-ichi appears to be a success. Stores offer fresh vegetables, fruit and many other items at bargain prices and in a festive atmosphere. Proprietors don *happi* coats and bawl out their bargains for the morning, whilst elsewhere there are *yakisoba* stalls and *mochi*-making parties. So much for standing in a queue at the supermarket!

One of the earliest asa-ichi to start up in recent years was the Nishi-Ogikubo Higashi Ginza shopping street market, which began in October 1975 and is still going strong. It's held on the third Sunday of each month from 8 a.m. to about 11 a.m., and is a short walk from the south exit of Nishi-Ogikubo Station on the JNR Chuo Line in Suginami Ward.

SETAGAYA WARD

Sangenjaya market, every first and third Sunday from 9 a.m. to 10 a.m. Near Sangenjaya Station on the Shin-Tamagawa Line.

ITABASHI WARD

Kami Itabashi market, every first Sunday from 7 a.m. to 9 a.m. along Minami-guchi Ginza. Near Kami Itabashi Station on the Tobu Tojo Line.

Akatsuka market, every second Sunday from 7 a.m. to 9 a.m. A 10-minute walk from Narimasu Station on the Tobu Tojo Line.

Itabashi Fudo-dori market, every third Sunday from 7 a.m. to 9 a.m. Near Itabashi Kuyakushomae Station on the Toei Mita subway line.

Hasune Chuo shopping street market, on the last Sunday of every month from 7 a.m. to 9 a.m. Near the west exit of Hasune Station on the Toei Mita subway line.

OTA WARD

Yasukata Shotengai market, every third Sunday from 9 a.m. to 10:30 a.m. Near Yaguchi no Watashi Station on the Mekama Line.

Shimomaruko Market, every third Sunday (except August) from 9 a.m. to 10 a.m. Near Shimomaruko Station on the Mekama Line.

SUMIDA WARD

Tachibana Ginza market, every fourth Sunday from 8 a.m. From Higashi-Azuma Station on the Tobu Kameido Line.

NERIMA WARD

Sakuradai Kita-guchi market, every first Sunday from 7 a.m. to 9 a.m. Near Sakuradai Station on the Seibu Ikebukuro Line.

ADACHI WARD

Towa Ginza Shotengai market, every second Sunday from 7 a.m. to 9 a.m. An 8-minute walk from Kameari Station on JNR Joban Line.

MEGURO WARD

Yutenji market, every fourth Sunday from 10 a.m.-noon. From Yutenji Station on the Tokyu Toyoko Line.

EDOGAWA WARD

Shokakuji market, on the 6th and 26th of each month, from 8 a.m. to noon. Old market held in precincts of a temple, dealing mainly in clothing. A 15-minute walk south from Kasai Station on the Tozai subway line.

TANASHI CITY

Tanashi market, held every first and third Sunday from 7 a.m. to 9 a.m. Mainly fresh vegetables. Along the road in front of the Nokyo Building, from Tanashi Station on the Seibu Shinjuku Line.

CHIBA PREFECTURE

Shofukuji market, a sister fair of Shokakuji, held on the 8th, 18th and 28th of each month from 8 a.m. to noon. A 13-minute walk south from Urayasu Station on the Tozai subway line. Again, mainly clothing.

Early risers get the best bargains.

Raking in the Money at Asakusa

トリの市

THE festive season starts early in Asakusa. Even before department stores have put up their Christmas trees, the *tori-no-ichi* fair has been held once, twice, and sometimes even three times.

This is a fair at which colorfully decorated rakes called *kumade* are sold. People come from far and near to the Otori Shrine, discarding the rakes which they bought the previous year and purchasing new ones in the hope that they will bring good luck and prosperity in the coming 12 months.

Otori Shrine has held this fair since the middle of the 18th century, although its origins are thought to go back to the first century when the third son of Emperor Taiko, Yamato Takeru no Mikoto, stopped at the shrine before going on to win an important battle. After his victory, he returned to the shrine and offered his thanks in the form of a bamboo rake.

His visit happened to be on a day of the cock *(tori no hi)* according to the lunar calendar, hence the fact that the fair is held on every day of the cock in November, of which there are either two or three.

Otori Shrine is a short walk from Minowa or Iriya stations on the Hibiya subway line, or from Minowa Station on the Arakawa tram line. At fair time, directions are usually posted at these stations, but you won't go wrong if you just follow the crowds. The streets are lined with stalls selling all kinds of goodies, and as you approach the shrine you'll hear the occasional burst of handclapping which is customarily made after a kumade is sold.

The rakes, which are decorated with various trinkets linked to good luck, come in a variety of sizes, the small ones costing about ¥1,500 (but usually knocked down to ¥1,000 or even less after a period of festive haggling), the larger ones fetching up to ¥100,000 and more.

Together with Asakusa's other famous year-end spectacle, the *hagoita* fair held December 17-19 in the grounds of Sensoji Temple, Otori Shrine's tori-no-ichi is one of those rare occasions when being jostled by crowds can be fun. The fair is held from midnight of the

A kumade rake heads
for a new home.

previous day through to midnight of the tori no hi, and the best time to go is after dark, when the displays of kumade rakes — and the red faces of the salespeople in their *happi* coats and *hachimaki* headbands — are lit up by light bulbs swaying in the evening breeze.

If for some reason you can't make it to Asakusa for the tori-no-ichi, or if you've been there before, then try one of the other main "cock" fairs. In Meguro, the Meguro Otori Shrine has had tori-no-ichi fairs since the 1830s. It's a 10-minute walk from JNR Meguro Station along Meguro Dori road in the direction of Yamate Dori avenue.

A much more recent fair is held at Shinjuku Hanazono Shrine, which is a short walk from the east exit of JNR Shinjuku Station, beyond Kinokuniya book store and near Shinjuku Ward Office. Check on the dates of forthcoming fairs, because the tori no hi falls on different days each year.

Black Eyes for Good Luck

ダルマ市

NEW Year celebrations in Japan are marked by the exchange of *nengajo* cards, an early start to see the first sunrise, the *hatsumode* visit to the local temple or shrine and the eating of special dishes called *osechi ryori.* Also part and parcel of the occasion are the *daruma ichi,* fairs at which daruma dolls are sold.

The daruma doll, usually colored red and white, is a symbol of good luck and perseverance. However often the doll is knocked over, it always manages to roll back into an upright position, and in this way symbolizes strength and fortune. Usually people take their old darumas along to the fair and throw them away at a designated spot before purchasing new ones.

A small daruma can be bought for between ¥300 and ¥1,000. It has no arms, no legs, and no eyes. The lack of arms and legs is connected with the legend of the priest who sat in meditation for nine years and lost the use of his limbs. The eyes are for you to paint in. First, the left eye, and as you apply the black paint, you make your wish. You can add the right eye when the wish comes true. Television often shows scenes of Japanese politicians painting in the missing eyes of daruma dolls after they have won an election.

The largest daruma fairs at New Year's take place at Haijima, Kawagoe and Takasaki, although smaller ones are also held here and there in December. The fair of Shofukuji Temple (better known as Iizumi Kannon) in Odawara, for example, is held every year on December 17 and 18.

The Haijima fair takes place at Haijima Daishi Temple on January 2 and 3, from early in the morning until evening. The extensive temple grounds, centering on a small lake, are crowded with stalls selling daruma dolls, candies, masks, spinning tops, *yakisoba* and much more on this festive occasion. A plant fair is also held there, and you can reach the temple in 20 minutes on foot from Akishima Station on the JNR Ome Line from Tachikawa.

The Kawagoe fair is held at Kitain Temple on January 3, and again on February 3. Like the Haijima Daishi fair, it is a very crowded but cheerful occasion as many people combine daruma-hunting with hatsumode, the first temple visit of the New Year. Kitain Temple is a 20-minute walk from Hon-Kawagoe Station on the Seibu Shinjuku Line or alternatively from Kawagoe Station on the Tobu Tojo Line from Ikebukuro.

The third of the big New Year daruma fairs takes place on January 6 and 7 at Shorinzan Daruma Temple in Takasaki, which can be reached by Gunma bus from Takasaki Station on the JNR Takasaki Line from Ueno.

Smaller daruma fairs are to be found in Ome City on January 12 and in Chichibu on January 12 and 13, but don't worry if you miss all of these New Year markets, because another daruma fair, and one of the most famous, is held at Jindaiji Temple in Chofu on March 3 and 4 every year. A multitude of stalls are set up along the approach roads to the temple and within its precincts. Jindaiji, with the Jindai Botanical Garden located nearby, is 15 minutes by bus from Chofu Station on the Keio Line from Shinjuku, and well worth a visit at any time.

Leisure Trips

Rambling Along the Enoden Line

江の電

A different approach to the well-known attractions of the Kamakura area is to use the local Enoden Line which links the former capital of Japan with Fujisawa. The Enoden Line started operating in 1902. There used to be a total of 41 stations along the line, but the number has been whittled down to 15 now.

It is a charming 34-minute journey. The two-coach train passes truly varied scenery, rambling down the middle of a road, squeezing between rows of houses, emerging for a short stretch by the sea, stopping at unmanned stations, and occasionally halting to allow the train coming from the opposite direction on the single-track line to pass by.

It takes about one hour to reach Fujisawa from Shinjuku by express train on the Odakyu Line. Enoden Station is across the road from Fujisawa Station, inside the Enoden Department Store.

Before setting out it is worth buying a "free pass" which covers the return journey between the station of purchase on the Odakyu Line and Fujisawa, plus as many rides as you like on the Enoden Line. This is the "B" ticket, and when purchased at Shinjuku it costs ¥910. There is also an "A" ticket available at ¥1,490 which includes use of Keihin Kyuko bus services as well.

The fourth station along the line from Fujisawa is Shonan Kaigan Koen, from where the Enoshima Aquarium and Marineland can be reached. These facilities are covered by a common ticket, and one of the three discount coupons which come with the Odakyu pass can be used there.

The other two discount coupons can be used for the Enoshima Escalator, which provides an easy ascent up to the shrine and observation point on the island, and the Enoshima Tropical Garden. Just to the northeast of Enoshima Station is Ryukoji Temple, the site where the priest Nichiren, founder of the Nichiren Sect, was saved from execution in the 13th century when his executioner's sword broke.

Next stop is Koshigoe Station, from where it is a short walk east to Mampukuji Temple, famous as the site where Minamoto Yoshitsune wrote a letter of allegiance after being banned from entering Kamakura by his brother, Yoritomo, in the 12th century.

Alighting at each and every station can be tiring, so it is advisable to take a break at this point and stroll along the seafront to the next station, Kamakurakoko-mae, and from there take the train to Kamakura at the end of the line to see Tsurugaoka Hachimangu Shrine, Zeniarai Benten Shrine and the host of other famous spots in the vicinity.

On the return journey along the Enoden Line you can stop off at Hase Station to see the Hase Kannon and the Kamakura Daibutsu (Great Buddha), and at Gokurakuji Station to see the temple of the same name.

Inamuragasaki Station provides a good finale for a day on the Enoden Line route. From the station, head for the sea, and to the east you'll see a cliff park called Inamuragasaki Point. This is a good place from where to view the sea and Enoshima Island, especially in early evening as the sun goes down and the coastline lights up.

Legend has it that from this cliff in 1333 a general of the imperial army tossed a golden sword into the ocean with a prayer that the tide would recede. It duly did so, and his army was able to pass by the foot of the cliff and rout its enemy in Kamakura.

From Inamuragasaki, the Enoden Line can be taken back to Fujisawa. Alternatively, walk along the seafront toward Enoshima, and from Katase-Enoshima Station take the Odakyu Line back to Shinjuku. Passes can be purchased at any Odakyu travel center and, being valid for two days, are suitable for both one-day and stopover trips. If you want to make an early start, buy your ticket before the day of departure, as the centers do not open until 10 a.m.

Letting Off Steam at Children's Land

こどもの国

BOARDING the train for Kodomo no Kuni at Nagatsuda Station in Kanagawa Prefecture is like getting on a school excursion special: it's packed with noisy young children all carrying small rucksacks and flasks and apparently with not a care in the world.

The train reaches its destination in just five minutes, and the children gush out to join all the others who have already arrived at Kodomo no Kuni (Children's Land), a sprawling area of wooded hills and grassy slopes designed especially to absorb all that pent-up energy.

Kodomo no Kuni was planned in 1959 in commemoration of an imperial wedding and the official opening took place on the annual Children's Day festival in May 1965.

The farm which is located in the eastern corner of the park will be of particular interest to youngsters visiting from urban areas, and also to foreigners from greener pastures who have forgotten what cows look — and smell — like.

"Come on. Come back over here," orders an elderly farm hand, and a sheep plods toward him. "I don't let them roam too far away," the gentleman explains, "because people feed them all sorts of rubbish and if they get ill, that's the end of them." He then beckons a small child in the crowd to come over and feel the sheep's woolly coat. "It's just like a scarf!"

From the cows and sheep it's on to a small children's zoo with rabbits and other playful animal friends, and then to the ponies which children can ride for ¥250.

After rounding off a visit to the farm with a cup of fresh milk, head north for Swan Lake, an artificial pond divided into two by a bobbing drum can bridge. One half of Swan Lake is for rowing boats and the other half for drum can rafts holding a maximum of six people. These rafts can be used free of charge and without time limit, although when a queue forms at the boarding point, people are asked to make do with about 10 minutes per ride.

Rural scenes at Kodomo no Kuni.

Other facilities available at Kodomo no Kuni include a skating rink in winter, swimming pools in summer, a rather rusty Hans Andersen memorial building, an old tramcar and fire engine for youngsters to clamber about on, a playground site with all kinds of slides and swings to test Tarzan skills, and a 1,600-meter cycling course with single bicycles and tandems available.

Also dotted about the park are various field athletic structures on which adults can rediscover forgotten muscles, while camellia, plum and cherry trees provide plenty of picturesque seasonal scenery. There is a restaurant near the entrance to Kodomo no Kuni, but the park offers plenty of space in which to enjoy family picnics.

Kodomo no Kuni is open every day except Mondays, from 9:30 a.m. to 4:30 p.m. When Monday is a national holiday, it closes on the following day instead. Entrance is ¥300 for adults and senior high school students, ¥100 for junior and elementary school pupils and ¥50 for infants.

It is reached by taking the Shin-Tamagawa Line from Shibuya to Nagatsuda, and changing to the Kodomo no Kuni Line for the 5-minute trip to the entrance.

Have your children wear clothes which you don't mind getting soiled and let them play to their heart's content. After a day of fun at Kodomo no Kuni, the return journey will be much quieter than the arrival was.

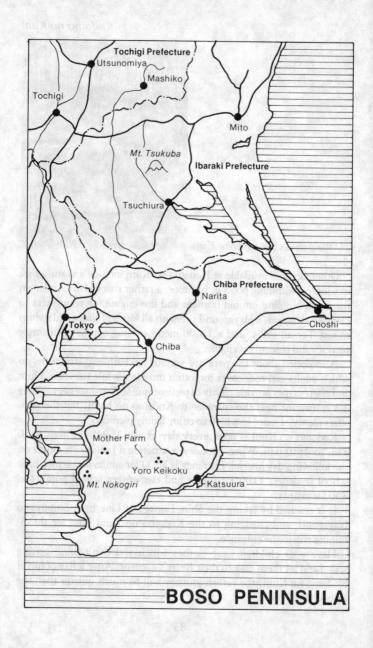

BOSO PENINSULA

Back to Narita for the Day

成田

MOST foreigners enter Japan by way of Narita in Chiba Prefecture, and rarely return there until the time comes to leave the country. Memories of long journeys and Customs checks are usually enough to stop people from wanting to venture in that direction on free weekends.

In fact, a trip to Narita turns up several unexpected attractions, both old and new. For the old, head for Narita Shinshoji Temple, about a 10-minute walk from JNR Narita Station. Turn right out of the wicket, and then left out of the station, and after picking up a map of the area (in Japanese) at the small tourist information office, follow the narrow road and signposts to Shinshoji.

The area which you pass through is a pretty seedy district of bars and clubs, but don't be put off. Eventually you reach a road lined with large souvenir shops and eating places more befitting a bustling temple town. Walk down this road and the temple entrance is on the left.

Narita Shinshoji Temple has its origins back in the 10th century. At the time of a rebellion by Taira no Masakado in the late 930s, Emperor Sujaku sent not only an expedition from Kyoto to Kanto to fight him, but also an image of Fudo, or Acala, the god of fire.

The image, said to have been carved by Kobo Daishi (774-835), was brought to a place near Narita and prayers were offered there until Masakado was killed in 940. A temple was then built to enshrine the image, and this was moved to the present site of Shinshoji (sometimes called Narita Fudo) in 1705.

The main hall of the temple was rebuilt in 1968 and is a large but rather unimpressive concrete affair. Offsetting this, however, are several structures of cultural and historic significance, including the Komyo-do Hall (built in 1701 as the main hall and moved to its present site just behind the new main hall in 1858 "using a rope of women's hair"); the temple *niomon* gate (built in 1830); and the Issaikyo Hall (first built in 1722 and rebuilt in 1809).

You'll soon recognize the latter hall because of the constant stream of people who enter and help keep the rotating library spinning round. The library contains the Buddhist scriptures and it is said that pushing the library round once is equivalent to reading all the scriptures.

To the right of this hall is the temple bell tower, and to the left a path which leads into Naritasan Park, 165,000 sq. meters of plum and cherry blossom trees, various other kinds of foliage, ponds, a waterfall, a small zoo, swans and turtles, and everything else you might want of a pleasant park.

The newest attraction in Narita is the Chiba Prefectural Flower Center, located near the northern tip of the airport. Buses do pass nearby, but they are few and far between, so it's perhaps best to take a taxi from Shinshoji. Ask for the Hana Ueki Center. It takes 15 minutes, and the fare will be about ¥2,000.

The surrounding wilderness and jets passing overhead don't make the best of environments, but the center itself is a refreshingly large and green park with a multitude of trees, plants and flowers on display and for sale, plenty of grass areas, model gardens and so on. Entrance is free, and the center is open from 9 a.m. to 4:30 p.m., and closed on Mondays.

To return to Narita by bus, turn right out of the main entrance and walk along the road to the crossroads, passing monuments to three policemen who died in battles over construction of the airport in 1971 on the way. The Toho bus stop for Chiba Kotsu buses is just to the left. It's a good idea to check the times of buses before entering the center.

Narita can be reached by the JNR Sobu Main Line from Tokyo or the Keisei Line from Ueno. For those wishing to extend their trips, the Sobu Main Line runs from Narita to Choshi, and the Kashima Line runs through Katori (for Katori Shrine) to Kashima (for Kashima Shrine).

Making Sure the World Is Round

銚子

IF you've ever had any doubts about the world being round, then there is one place in Chiba Prefecture which will put your mind at rest for good — Mount Atago in Choshi. This "mountain" is in fact only 84.6 meters tall, but it is still the highest point on the Choshi Peninsula.

Anyone standing in the mountain's observation tower gets an unbroken view of the surrounding world. The view is spectacular because 330 degrees of one's vision is taken up by the Pacific Ocean, and indeed part of the remaining 30 degrees is occupied by a large lake, so that one actually gets an almost 360-degree panorama of water.

Follow the horizon around and — yes indeed! — the globe appears to be circular, and you'll understand why the top of Mount Atago is called the Chikyu no Maruku Mieru Tenbodai (Observation Point for Seeing the World Round).

There are two other special attractions at this easternmost end of Kanto, and both can be observed well by using the telescopes (¥100) on the observation platform. Focus to the west and you'll see what's known as the Japanese "Dover," a 12-km stretch of perpendicular cliffs called Byobugaura. It gets its Japanese name from its appearance as a long screen *(byobu)*.

Focus to the east and you'll spot the shining white lighthouse on Inubo Cape, built in 1874 by an Englishman, Richard Henry Branton.

Choshi

In order to see these sights at close quarters, head for Choshi, which is reached in about two hours from Tokyo Station by the JNR Sobu Main Line express. From bus stop No. 3 outside Choshi Station, a bus leaves for the local Kokumin Shukusha (national lodge: Inubo Hotel), which is a convenient place to stay at 4,800 for one night, including two meals. Reservations should be made beforehand, by calling 0479-22-3205 (in Japanese).

Other arrangements to stay overnight can be made at the two information offices at Choshi Station. Try and get a place near the sea, like the Kokumin Shukusha, because the promenade path leading along the seafront, up to and past the lighthouse, makes for a pleasant evening stroll.

Inubozaki Lighthouse, Mount Atago and Byobugaura are all within fairly easy walking distance of the Kokumin Shukusha, but if possible rent a bicycle. The Kokumin Shukusha provides cycles at ¥200 for two hours and ¥100 extra for every hour after that.

First stop should be the 51.8-meter-high lighthouse, entrance to which is ¥50. From there, turn left at the main road, and then right, and keep going until you cross the railway line. Turn left at the next junction, and then right just beyond the gasoline station, and Mount Atago lies ahead of you.

The road goes up to the observation platform. After confirming that the world is round, take the road going down in the opposite direction from which you came. When you reach another main road, turn right, and then left under the expressway, and eventually you come to the Dover of the East.

To return to the Kokumin Shukusha, go back to the main road under the expressway, and instead of turning left for Mount Atago, keep straight on through Narai Port and back in the direction of the lighthouse.

It is possible to return to Choshi by bus, but a trip on the local one-coach Choshi Electric Railway has become something of a "must" with the recent "local line boom." The terminus of this line is Togawa, an eight-minute walk from the Kokumin Shukusha, and it reaches Choshi in 20 minutes. Alternatively, Inubo Station on the same line is a 10-minute walk from Inubozaki in the direction of Mount Atago.

Down to the Bottom of the Sea

勝浦

CHILDREN love a trip to the seaside and the chance it gives them for a romp in the sand, a paddle and maybe even a boat ride. They might also appreciate a look at what goes on below the surface.

This experience can be enjoyed at Katsuura, on the east coast of Boso Peninsula, where jutting out into the sea is a marine tower which reaches 8.5 meters down into the ocean. At the bottom of the tower there is a circular room with 24 windows from which visitors can observe the fish, sea plants and rocks on the sea bottom. The tower, which holds 50 people, was opened in 1980 as part of the Katsuura Kaichu Koen Park.

Illustrations in the observation room help identify the fish, mainly *ishidai* (parrot fish), *kawahagi* (filefish), *hakofugu* (spotted trunk fish), *mejina* (opaleye) and *utsubo* (moray). There are unfortunately no explanations in English, although more pictorial displays can be found in the tower's exhibition room and in the nearby Visitor Center.

The marine tower at Katsuura Kaichu Ko-en Park

Wares spread out on the street . . . and a well-prepared customer. (Right)

The tower is open from 8:30 a.m. until 6 p.m. in summer, and from 9 a.m. until 5 p.m. during the rest of the year, with no holidays. Entrance is ¥900 for adults, ¥450 for junior high and elementary school children, and ¥200 for pre-school children over the age of four.

The marine park is a 10-minute bus ride from Katsuura Station, although buses are few so it might be wise to take a taxi. Alternatively, the park can be reached in 10 minutes on foot from Ubara Station, one stop along from Katsuura.

After visiting the tower, turn right out of the marine park and the road takes you through a tunnel and round to a small picturesque cove called Onaura in which stands a large rock with a hole in it. From there you can see Katsuura Lighthouse on the opposite side of Katsuura Bay, and it is in this direction that children might want to be taken next, for just beyond the lighthouse is a monkey park.

The best way to get there is to return to Katsuura Station by bus or taxi and then walk along the seafront toward the lighthouse. The road passes below the lighthouse and then up to the park. This area was the site of Katsuura Castle from the 10th to the 16th centuries. A small amusement ground is now the center of attention, together with the monkeys which roam about freely.

Katsuura is also famous for its four-centuries-old morning fish and fresh vegetable market. It is held on every day of the week except Wednesdays, from about 6 a.m. until noon. From the station, take the road to the left leading under the "welcome" sign, turn right when you come to a main road and keep walking until you reach the market street.

At the far end is Koshoji Temple, and in its grounds a huge gingko tree which has sprouted some 60 aerial roots and is a truly amazing spectacle. A prayer offered here is said to help mothers who have trouble breast-feeding their babies.

Katsuura can be reached in about 1 hour 50 minutes from Tokyo Station on the JNR Sotobo Line express. It is a neighboring city of Onjuku and Ohara, two other popular resorts in the area.

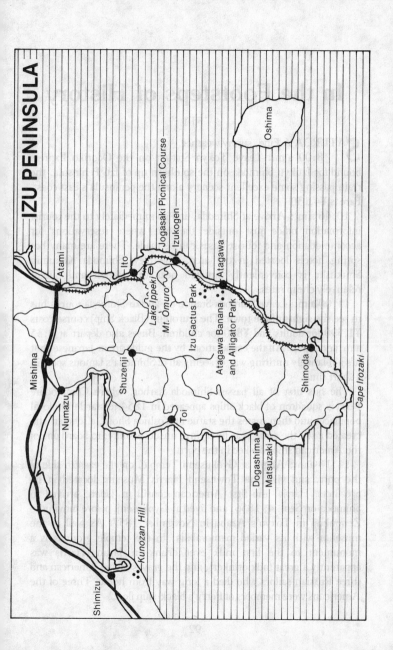

IZU PENINSULA

Oshima

Atami

Ito

Jogasaki Picnical Course

Izukogen

Lake Ippeki

Mt. Ōmuro

Izu Cactus Park

Atagawa

Atagawa Banana
and Alligator Park

Mishima

Shuzenji

Numazu

Toi

Shimoda

Cape Irozaki

Dogashima

Matsuzaki

Shimizu

Kunozan Hill

In the Footsteps of History

下田

SATURDAY. Fine, sunny weather.

8:00 a.m.: Leave Tokyo Station on the Odoriko Express bound for Izukyu-Shimoda on the southern tip of Izu Peninsula, the train passing some excellent scenery along the peninsula's east coast. Fare is ¥4,130.

10:46 a.m.: Arrive at Shimoda, and go immediately to the tourist information office just outside the exit where reservations for accommodation and tourist buses can be made. There are many hot spring hotels located in the area. The New Shimoda Kokumin Shukusha is conveniently situated near the station and quotes relatively cheap rates.

11:00 a.m.: Leave Shimoda Station on an Izu-Shimoda tourist bus to see the sights of the town. The Kurofune (Black Ship) course costs ¥1,590 for adults and ¥880 for children. Buses also depart at 9:35 a.m. and 2 p.m. All the explanations by the guide are in Japanese, but it's a relatively untiring way of seeing all of Shimoda's famous spots in a short time.

The bus first of all passes Shimoda harbor, where Commodore Perry's squadron of black ships appeared in 1854 to startle the local populace, and then passes the statue of Yoshida Shoin, a scholar who created a stir the same year by trying, unsuccessfully, to board one of the American ships docked in the port.

11:10 a.m.: Alight at Gyokusenji Temple, on the eastern side of the port, and visit the Townsend Harris Museum located in its precincts. Harris, the first American consul in Japan, arrived in Shimoda on Sept. 4, 1856, and lived at Gyokusenji before moving to Zenpukuji in Tokyo's Azabu in November 1857. As well as the museum with its varied memorabilia, in the temple grounds is a monument to the first milk ever drunk in Japan (Harris was apparently a great milk drinker), and the graves of five American and three Russian sailors who died a long way from home. Three of the Americans were members of Perry's black-ship fleet.

The black ship model outside Shimoda Station.

The bus then heads for Cape Tsumekizaki, famous for its views of the ocean, its lighthouse, and its narcissus flowers which blossom in winter. Time is taken here for a souvenir group photo and a short rest.

11:55 a.m.: The bus leaves Tsumekizaki and returns to Shimoda Port, where participants in the course transfer to a small tourist boat modeled after the black ships for a trip around the harbor. The island with the red torii arch, located near the shore, is Bentenjima. It was from here that Yoshida, together with one companion, rowed out to the Perry fleet, only to be unceremoniously turned away. His purpose in approaching the ships is not altogether clear.

12:30 p.m.: Back to the bus, which then sets off for Ryosenji Temple in the western part of Shimoda. This temple is the site where the Shimoda Treaty between America and Japan was signed in 1854. These days it is also well known for its Treasure House of phallic deities, dildos and other such symbols. Entrance to the latter costs an extra ¥200.

12:50 p.m.: After Ryosenji, the bus drops in at Hofukuji Temple to see the grave and museum of Okichi, Townsend Harris' attendant and, it is said, lover.

The story goes that Okichi, a geisha, was forced to end her affair with another man in order to become Harris' maid at Gyokusenji. The relationship developed, and Okichi accompanied Harris when he moved to Edo (Tokyo). After Harris returned to America in 1862, she met her former lover again, but their marriage ended in separation. Thereafter Okichi led an unhappy life, drinking excessively, and in 1890 she drowned herself.

It is difficult to say what is fact and what is fiction in the Okichi legend, but the incense sticks burning at her grave are sufficient evidence of the continued attention paid to her.

1:15 p.m.: The bus leaves Hofukuji for the Mount Nesugata ropeway. This is the end of the course. The bus ticket is good for a return journey on the ropeway, and as much time as desired can be spent on the top of the mountain, enjoying the vews of the port city from above and visiting Shimoda Memorial Hall. The latter contains items related to Shimoda's history collected by a local citizen, Fusui Mori (1901-61), and is particularly interesting for the material exhibited on the Russian squadron led by Eufimii Putyatin which entered Shimoda in October 1854.

Among the items displayed are a travel bag used by Putyatin and a glass said to have been presented to him by the czar at the time, Nicholas I.

2:30 p.m.: Descend the mountain by ropeway, and then walk over to the western side of the harbor to visit Shimoda Park with its wild bird forest and aquarium. Finish the day's agenda by walking along the park's 2,400-meter "health course," passing the aquarium on the way, and then returning to the center of Shimoda.

(The Okichi Festival of Hofukuji Temple takes place every year on March 27 from about 10 a.m. until 3 p.m. Shimoda's Kurofune Festival, commemorating the arrival of Perry's black ships, is held annually from May 16-18.)

94

From Coast to Coast

伊豆半島

MOST people enter the Izu Peninsula via Atami, either traveling straight on down the east coast from there in the direction of Shimoda, or heading directly for their reserved hot spring accommodation. If time is available, however, it is well worth exploring the peninsula's coastline at a more leisurely pace.

The first stop can be Atami itself and a visit to the MOA Art Museum, opened with much fanfare in January 1982. It offers a standing exhibition of Japanese pottery, lacquerware, calligraphy and painting, as well as regular special exhibitions and works by Western artists. The museum is an 8-minute bus ride from Atami Station.

From Atami, a boat may be taken to Hatsushima, Tokyo's closest Pacific island situated just 10 km and 23 minutes away. There was once a custom on this island that in order to keep the number of households from increasing, all sons except the eldest had to go to the mainland.

The population of Hatsushima is still less than 300, but in recent years the island has become a popular tourist spot and during the summer months especially the number of visitors surpasses that figure many times over.

Hatsushima has a circumference of just 4 km and can easily be covered in a day, although night views of Atami over the water make an extended stay well worthwhile. The island's main attractions in the daytime are the rather commercialized Hatsushima Vacationland and the seasonal foliage.

From Hatsushima, a boat can be taken to Ito, just down the coast from Atami and a convenient place to stay overnight. Ito is a small town boasting a significant place in history. It was there that William Adams, the first Englishman to set foot in Japan, lived from 1605 to 1610. Miura Anjin, as Adams was called by the Japanese, helped build Japan's first Western-style ships in the port there.

Using Ito as a base, there are many places of interest to see in the area. If it's history you're looking for, take a walk along the seafront

Dogashima cliffs.   Renchakuji Temple.

and, near the place from where boats go to Hatsushima, you'll find a monument to Adams, and another related one erected by the poet Edmund Blunden "To the Citizens of Ito."

If it's hiking you want, there is an excellent 9-km course along the Jogasaki coastline, formed by volcanic eruptions of nearby Mount Omuro in the distant past. The first 3 km is called the Jogasaki Picnical Course, the entrance to which is a 40-minute bus ride from Ito Station. Take the bus bound for Kaiyo Koen ocean park and get off at the Jogasakiguchi bus stop (¥460).

From the bus stop, follow the narrow road which leads toward the sea and you come to the course's signposted entrance. The path then takes you past a thatched cottage which is now a restaurant but in the Edo Period was the site of a base for local mullet fishermen. From there, the course follows the jagged coastline as far as a 48-meter-long suspension bridge, and after crossing this you emerge at the car park for Kaiyo Koen ocean park.

Five minutes' walk away is Renchakuji Temple. After visiting the main hall, follow the path leading to the inner hall, and the steps going up behind this take you onto the Jogasaki Shizen Kenkyuro (nature trail).

This course follows the coastline for a further 6 km, and crosses another suspension bridge on the way. Fewer people seem to tackle this second part of the Jogasaki course, although if anything the views and sounds of the sea are even more breathtaking.

From the end of the course, it is a 15-minute walk to Izu Kogen Station for trains back to Ito. Near the station is the Jogasaki Bunka Shiryokan, a museum displaying various items of local historic and folkloric interest and some particularly notable pictures made of glass.

If it's flowers you want, head for the Izu Cactus Park, also a 40-

Sign for the Picnical Course.   Dogashima harbor.

minute bus ride from Ito Station, or the nearby Mount Komuro Park, famous for its azaleas which blossom in April. The Cactus Park contains cactus plants from around the world as well as a small zoo. Entrance is ¥1,000.

Other attractions near the Cactus Park include the Ikeda Museum of 20th Century Art, the 581-meter-high Mount Omuro which can be ascended by means of a tourist lift, and Lake Ippeki, which offers boating facilities.

After Ito, the next stop down the spa-studded coast might be Atagawa, the journey taking 30 minutes by Izu Kyuko Railway. In front of the station is the Atagawa Banana and Alligator Park which utilizes local hot spring water to cultivate tropical plants and rear alligators.

From Atagawa, it's about 30 minutes by train to Shimoda, the historic port town on the south coast of the 60-km-long peninsula.

Buses can be taken from Shimoda to various places on Izu's west coast. The Tokai tourist bus, for example, links Shimoda with Mishima on the Shinkansen Line via Cape Irozaki and Dogashima, with stops at the former to see the Irozaki Jungle Park and at the latter for lunch. The journey can also be made by ordinary bus routes, which would allow more time to explore Irozaki and to take a turbulent boat ride past, around and under the cliffs of Dogashima. There are also boat services operating between Shimoda and Cape Irozaki and between Matsuzaki, Dogashima, and Numazu.

Japanese National Railways offers special tickets for the Izu Peninsula which allow use of JNR and private trains and buses as many times as you want during a four-day period. The pass can be purchased at any main JNR station and costs about ¥9,000, depending on which station you depart from.

Tokyo's 'Hawaiian Island'

大島

OSHIMA, the largest of the seven islands of Izu, lies about 120 km south of Tokyo. The two symbols of the island are its camellia flowers which blossom in January and February, and Mount Mihara, an active volcano situated in the center of the island.

Sightseeing bus tours on Oshima are scheduled such that it is possible to make a day trip to the island from Tokyo. Overnight boats leave from Takeshiba Pier near Hamamatsucho Station on the JNR Yamanote Line at 10 p.m. and reach Motomachi, Oshima's main port, at about 5 in the morning. It is then possible to take a rest and have breakfast in a local *ryokan* or *minshuku* before catching a sightseeing bus which will speed you around the island's main tourist spots and get you back to the port, either Motomachi or Okada, from where boats leave for Tokyo in the afternoon.

A package tour of this type costs about ¥8,500 but, unless you are really pressed for time, should probably be avoided. There are enough things to see on Oshima to justify at least one night's stay there. Arriving by night boat from Tokyo is a popular course, but there is also usually a morning boat, and services operate from Yokohama, Atami and Ito as well. The journey by fast boat from Atami takes just 1 hour and 10 minutes.

There is an information center in Motomachi which will help with accommodation if you have not made reservations beforehand. Oshima has several modern hotels and ryokan inns, a Kokumin Shukusha lodge in Motomachi, and a couple of youth hostels.

Motomachi is situated on the west coast of the 91 sq. km island. Three km to the north is Oshima Airport, from where Haneda Airport in Tokyo can be reached in about 40 minutes. In the vicinity of the airport are several of the island's main tourist spots, including the Izu Oshima Hawaiian Botanical Garden, the Oshima Local History Museum, a Squirrel Village, a Folk Entertainment Museum and the Oshima Milk Center.

Oshima has a sister-island relationship with Hawaii, and the botanical garden displays many kinds of plants from that island — including hibiscus and bougainvillea — and from other places around the world.

On the northernmost tip of the island are the capes of Chigasaki and Kazahayazaki, with Oshima Lighthouse standing on the latter. Fine views can be had from these places of the Izu, Boso and Miura peninsulas on the mainland, and on a clear day Mount Fuji is said to be a wonderful sight from there.

The main attraction on the east coast is the Shizen Dobutsu Koen (Oshima Zoo Park), where a large variety of plants and animals, including monkeys, are kept. On the south coast, the picturesque port of Habu is worth a visit.

Sightseeing buses take in most of these places. Regular buses also operate, and bicycles can be rented if you decide on a cycling tour of the island. Mount Mihara can be reached by bus from Motomachi. From the terminus at Mihara-guchi, it is a 35-minute walk along a specially made tourist route up to the crater observation point. The desert-like lava bed around Mount Mihara (758 meters high) contrasts sharply with the rich foliage observed elsewhere on the island.

Second-class boat fares to Oshima are ¥2,550 from Tokyo, ¥2,500 from Yokohama, ¥1,850 from Atami and ¥1,630 from Ito. The high-speed service from Atami costs ¥4,000. When weather conditions necessitate, boats arrive at and leave from the port of Okada in the north instead of Motomachi.

Visiting the Other Toshogu Shrine

久能山

SATURDAY. Cloudy at first, becoming fine later.

8:16 a.m.: Leave Tokyo Station by Shinkansen Kodama train for Shizuoka. Fare is ¥4,300.

9:52 a.m.: Arrive at Shizuoka Station.

9:58 a.m.: Catch a bus from bus stop No. 1-2 in front of the station for Kunozan-shita (¥320). It's a pleasant journey along the sea front.

10:32 a.m.: Arrive at Kunozan-shita terminus. Cross the road and have a small snack by the sea before heading for Toshogu Shrine.

10:50 a.m.: Set off for the shrine on Kunozan hill (270 meters high). Walk past fields where strawberries are being grown for the January-May picking season toward the stone steps which can be seen winding their way up to the shrine. There are 1,159 steps altogether. It's a short but steep climb, with plenty of resting places from where the view of the sea can be enjoyed.

11:16 a.m.: Reach the gateway to Kunozan Toshogu Shrine.

11:20 a.m.: Arrive at the entrance to the shrine. Tickets for both the shrine and its museum cost ¥450. Toshogu Shrine was built in 1617 by the second Tokugawa shogun, Hidetada, in honor of his father, Ieyasu, the first shogun. The latter's remains were buried there before being taken to Nikko, and a stone grave built in 1640 is located behind the main shrine building. The path leading to it is lined by some fine stone lanterns.

The red-lacquered shrine benefits from being on a more modest scale than its counterpart in Nikko, built 19 years later, while the museum contains many precious items, including the oldest foreign-made clock extant in Japan, a present to Ieyasu from the Mexican governor-general. It was made in Madrid in 1581.

12:20 p.m.: Take the ropeway from Kunozan across the valley to the Nihondaira Plateau (6 minutes), a spot dominated by pinball machines and television towers. Eat lunch, then search for Mount Fuji and the Izu Peninsula, both of which, judging from the postcards, present excellent spectacles when viewed from here.

The twisting pathway up
Kunozan hill.

Unfortunately, both are wrapped in haze.

1:33 p.m.: Catch the Shimizu-bound bus from Nihondaira. The
driver slows the bus on the way down the hill to give passengers a
better look at the *mikan* orange groves.

1:53 p.m.: Alight at Baiinjimae bus stop (fare ¥290). Baiinji
Temple, in the grounds of which are the grave, statue and small
museum of Shimizu no Jirocho, lies just around the corner to the left.
Entrance is ¥200. Jirocho (1820-93) was a local gang leader turned
philanthropist who did much for the area, and his birthplace is located
a short walk from the temple.

2:20 p.m.: Leave Baiinji, cross the road, turn left at the traffic
signal, and keep walking for about 10 minutes, past some fine old
timber buildings. Jirocho's birthplace is just to the right, across a
shopping street. The entrance way is now a souvenir shop, but you
can walk through and have a look in the back.

2:50 p.m.: Turn right out of the shop, then right again, and head
for Shimizu harbor.

3:40 p.m.: Leave for a trip around the harbor on a Shizuoka Kanko
Kisen boat. Fare is ¥800.

4:10 p.m.: The boat approaches the pine grove of Miho, and
Mount Fuji comes into view at last, albeit still shrouded in haze.

4:32 p.m.: Boat returns to the harbor. From there, cross the
railway track, then the road, and walk a few meters to the left for the
bus stop.

4:44 p.m.: Catch a bus for Shimizu Station (¥100).

4:55 p.m.: Rush to catch the next express train back to Tokyo.

A Little Lesson in Gardening

川口

TOKYO is not lacking when it comes to parks and gardens, but what is missing is contact with the act of cultivation itself. At first sight, Kawaguchi in Saitama Prefecture doesn't appear to be the place to go for this. Excepting a brief respite as the train passes over the Arakawa River, the view on both sides of the Keihin Tohoku Line is completely urban, and the area around Kawaguchi Station also provides little sign of greenery.

In fact, however, Kawaguchi is the starting point for visiting two prosperous centers of plant life which, when taken together, provide a refreshing day's outing from Tokyo. From the east exit of Kawaguchi Station take the bus bound for Shinmachi which passes the Kawaguchi Municipal Green Center. The ride takes about 15 minutes, and the bus stops outside the center's main gate.

The Green Center was opened in 1967 with the three objectives of promoting agriculture, improving young people's knowledge of the natural sciences, and providing a pleasant recreation spot. Now many people, and especially young families, can be seen examining the names of trees and plants around the park and in the large greenhouse, or enjoying a picnic on the extensive lawn.

The focal point of the center is a gigantic waterfall fountain which is turned on four times a day for 30 minutes at a time (at 10:00, 11:30, 13:30 and 15:00, although only at 11:30 and 13:30 in winter). Other attractions to be enjoyed while walking around the park include an azalea hill, iris, hydrangea, sasanqua and camellia areas, a "Swan Lake," and cactus plants in the greenhouse.

Near the main entrance potted plants, flowers and bonsai plants are sold, together with garden implements, fertilizer and so on. The Green Center is open from 9 a.m. until 5 p.m. every day except Tuesdays and the days following a weekday national holiday. Entrance is ¥200 for adults and ¥100 for children and students.

Just 4 km to the east is Angyo, a nursery village which claims to be the country's leading plant-growing area. There are no buses running

102

The large greenhouse at Kawaguchi Green Center.

The waterfall fountain.

between the two sites, but the distance can be covered in about 10 minutes by taxi. Ask the driver for the Angyo Mihonen and he'll drop you off at the model garden which is the focal point of the village. There is a pedestrian bridge linking the two sides of the garden across the road. The model garden is open from 9 a.m. until 4 p.m. every day and entrance is free. It is closed during the New Year period.

Various kinds of plants and tress grow in the garden, and the nearby Shokubutsu Shinko Center offers advice on cultivation. From there you can walk along the road and in and out of the many private nurseries which specialize in various branches of horticulture — bonsai plants, pines and maples to list but some — and welcome visitors.

Angyo has been a horticultural center for over three centuries, most of its products going to the Tohoku and Tokyo districts. Prices are generally lower than in town.

From the bus stop on the road going past the model garden, buses leave for Nishi-Kawaguchi Station on the Keihin Tohoku Line, the journey taking about 35 minutes.

Gunma's Very Own 'Fuji-san'

榛名湖

LAKE Haruna in Gunma Prefecture remains frozen over from December until late March, but this doesn't stop the tourists from coming. While some arrive to take advantage of the skating courses which are set up on the icy surface, others bring their fishing tackle.

Looked at from a distance, the lake presents quite a picture-postcard appearance in the winter, with skaters waltzing around in one area and fishermen poring over the small holes they have made in the ice in the hope of catching some *wakasagi* (pond smelt) in another.

From April the scene changes completely. Skates, and go-karts which also utilize the frozen surface in winter, give way to boats of various kinds and sizes. And Mount Haruna, the general name for a number of peaks bordering the lake, is officially opened to climbers from May 5.

Lake Haruna occupies the caldera of the most prominent of these now extinct volcanic peaks, called Haruna-Fuji because of its resemblance in shape to Mount Fuji. The lake has a 6-km circumference and is 1,084 meters above sea level. Haruna-Fuji, rising to 1,391 meters, is on the lake's east side, and Mount Kamondake (1,448 meters) is on the west.

There are plenty of hiking courses in the area, one popular route taking in nearby Mount Tenmoku, Matsunosawa Pass and Mount Soma (1,411 meters). Another route covers Mount Kamondake, the summit of which can be reached from the lakeside in about one hour.

The most common course for day trippers, however, involves a stroll around the lakeside and either a 50-minute climb up Haruna-Fuji or a 3-minute ride on its 483-meter-long ropeway.

Lake Haruna can be reached in 95 minutes by Gunma bus from bus stop No. 8 outside Takasaki Station. There is one bus every hour, convenient ones leaving Takasaki at 8:30, 9:30 and 10:30 a.m.

Near the lakeside bus stop there are several souvenir shops and places where skates and fishing equipment can be rented in winter, and bicycles hired during the rest of the year. There is also a horsedrawn buggy service operated in summer, shuttling people between the lake and the foot of the ropeway.

A short bus ride away from the lake, on the route to Takasaki, is Haruna Shrine. Founded in 585, the shrine is tucked away on the mountainside and occupies a large area noted for its magnificent cedar trees and rocks.

To reach the shrine, get off at the Haruna Jinja bus stop, walk back a short way in the direction from which the bus came, and take the road going up to the right until you reach the shrine's torii arch. The path beyond the arch leads first to a wooden three-storey pagoda dating from the late Edo Period (1603-1867), and then up to the main shrine buildings, passing a fine waterfall on the way. The colorful main hall dates from the late 18th century.

The shrine's festival takes place May 8-15 every year, while the lake holds an annual festival on the first Saturday in August.

Haruna Prefectural Park, centering on the lake, Haruna-Fuji and the shrine, can be visited in one day from Tokyo. For those who want to cover the sights in the area at a leisurely pace, however, there is plenty of accommodation available.

Haruna Shrine.

The Kokumin Shukusha lodge (tel.: 02737-4-9106) and youth hostel (tel.: 02737-4-9300) offer relatively cheap rates. Reservations for *ryokan* inns and *minshuku* in the area can be made by calling the Lake Haruna Tourist Association at 02737-4-9355. All such telephone inquiries should be made in Japanese.

For campers, there are two grounds open during the summer, the Mayumigaoka Camp Ground (tel.: 02737-4-9518) and the Haruna Lodge Camp Ground (tel.: 02737-4-9516).

Another common course is to link a visit to the Haruna area with a stopover at the nearby Ikaho hot spring resort, located to the east of Lake Haruna and reached in 40 minutes by Tobu bus from Shibukawa Station on the JNR Joetsu Line, or in 80 minutes by Gunma bus from Takasaki Station. It takes about 35 minutes to reach Ikaho from Lake Haruna by Gunma bus.

As well as its hot springs, Ikaho boasts a shrine (Ikaho Jinja), a ropeway leading up to Ikaho Highland observation point, and the Roka Memorial Hall, dedicated to Kenjiro Tokutomi (pen name Roka), the novelist who often visited the area and who helped make Ikaho a popular tourist spot by setting one of his novels there.

To reserve accommodation in the Ikaho hot spring area, call the Ikaho Onsen Tourist Association at 02797-2-3151, again preferably in Japanese. For information on reservations in English, contact your local Japan Travel Bureau office.

Schools, Sculpture and Wasabi

松本

MOST of Japan's centers of imported Western culture are located by the sea, notable examples being Yokohama, Kobe, Nagasaki and Hakodate, which all developed in the late 19th century as trading ports.

Western influences in Japan are not limited to the coastline, however. The visitor to Matsumoto, situated in the heart of Nagano Prefecture in an area often called the "roof of Japan," will find standing nearby the town's famous castle one of the finest examples of Meiji-Period architecture still remaining.

This is the former Kaichi School building, constructed in 1876 by a carpenter called Kiyoshige Tateishi. That it was built so soon after the Meiji Restoration in 1868 attests to the rapid spread of foreign influence in the regions, and to the enthusiasm for education in Nagano Prefecture.

The two-storey wooden structure is now a museum of educational history, with many materials on display related to the history of the school and the development of modern education in Japan. Of particular interest are the many old photographs and textbooks which can be seen in the exhibition rooms. The school is open every day in the April-October period, and closed on Sundays and national holidays between November and March. Visiting hours are from 8:30 a.m. to 5:30 p.m.

Another example of foreign influence can be found at the Rokuzan Museum, located in the Azumino area to the northwest of Matsumoto. The red-brick museum building is built in the style of a small European church and it contains the most important works of the sculptor Morie Ogiwara, whose professional name was Rokuzan.

Ogiwara (1879-1910), who was born in the area, went to the United States in 1901 to study art. He later moved to France and took up sculpture after seeing Rodin's "The Thinker." Ogiwara is credited with introducing Rodin's works to Japan, and his own "Woman" and "Miner" seem to have been influenced by the French sculptor's style. Both are exhibited in the museum, which is open every day except Mondays.

The Rokuzan Museum can be reached from Hotaka Station, about 30 minutes from Matsumoto on the JNR Oito Line. Bicycles can be rented in front of the station and the usual course takes in the museum, the Wasabi Farm where horseradish plants are grown, exhibited and sold (said to be the largest such farm in Japan), Hotaka Shrine, which despite its mountainous location holds a Ship Festival every September 26-27, and Tokoji Temple with its giant *geta* clogs, which are supposed to make wishes come true for anyone who stands on them.

The area is also famous for its roadside *dosojin* statues, of which there are 126 in the Hotaka district alone. Dating from the 19th century, they depict couples holding hands and are dedicated to traffic safety and marital bliss.

Roadside statues in Hotaka.

Back in Matsumoto, still to be seen are the castle and its Folklore Museum, the Matsumoto Mingeikan with its displays of local glassware and furniture, the Ukiyoe Museum and the Judicial Museum. Bicycles can be rented from several cycle shops near the station.

The Hotaka district is a popular day-trip destination from Matsumoto. Another is the Utsukushigahara Plateau, which can be reached in 1 hour 10 minutes by bus from the Matsumoto Bus Terminal. The highest point on the plateau is Ogato Peak, which rises to 2,034 meters. Also in the area is the Utsukushigahara Art Museum, a sister-museum of Hakone's Chokoku no Mori which similarly has an outdoor sculpture display. Utsukushigahara and Asama spas are situated on the bus route between Matsumoto and the plateau.

Matsumoto can be reached in about 3 hours 30 minutes by special express on the JNR Chuo Main Line from Shinjuku Station in Tokyo.

A Town With a 'Kurashiki Look'
栃木

THE Uzuma River flows through the town of Tochigi from north to south, and in the 17th and 18th centuries was the source of the area's prosperity. Hemp, timber, paper, grain, rice, coal, tobacco . . . all roads in the northern Kanto area led to Tochigi, from where goods would be loaded onto boats for shipment via the Uzuma to Edo (Tokyo).

The town originally developed as a castle town, but its fortress only stood for a short time, from 1591 until 1609. After that it began to develop as a distribution link between the northern districts of Japan and Edo, and as an important post-town conveniently located between Nikko and the capital. Tochigi also had a large horse market, with horses brought from the Tohoku area for auction to people in Edo.

Tochigi maintained its prosperous role until toward the end of the Meiji Period. It was indeed the capital of the prefecture from 1871 until 1884, after which Utsunomiya took over but the name remained the same: Tochigi Prefecture.

Now the Uzuma is a quiet river inhabited by numerous carp, but although there are no boats to be seen anymore, it remains the source of the town's attraction as a tourist spot. For a long time Tochigi has been overlooked as a result of the prominence of Nikko nearby, but with the recent boom in popularity of places with an old-town look, Tochigi's "Kurashiki appearance" has meant an increasing number of tourists visiting there. The focal point is the river, with willow trees planted along one bank and warehouse structures still standing on the other.

Tochigi is most easily reached by the Tobu Nikko Line from Tobu Asakusa Station in Tokyo. Express trains bound for Nikko don't stop at Tochigi, but the *kaisoku* limited express trains do, the journey taking about 80 minutes. Tochigi is also located on the JNR Ryomo Line running between Takasaki and Oyama.

As you emerge from the station, there is a small tourist

information office to the left where you can pick up a detailed pictorial guide map (in Japanese). There is also a large tourist map displayed near the station exit which shows the usual walking route around the town taking in the Tsukada Museum, the Yokoyama Local History Museum, the Tochigi Mingeikan, the Meiji-style former prefectural government building with its picturesque moat, and the Okada Kinenkan.

The Tsukada family were timber wholesalers in the district from 1844, and the warehouse museum contains several items of historic interest, particularly the large local festival float which is displayed there. Entrance to the museum is ¥300, and it is open from 9:30 a.m. to 5 p.m.

The starting point for the walking course is the Tochigi Catholic Church, reached by taking the road leading perpendicularly away from the station and then turning left. From the church, cross the narrow river, turn right, and then just keep walking along the road by the river. You'll soon come to the black fencing of the storehouses located on the opposite bank, indicating the location of the Tsukada Museum.

The old prefectural building and moat (above), and riverside warehouses.

110

It takes about an hour to see the architectural attractions of Tochigi. A good day's outing might cover the town in the morning, and nearby Mount Ohira in the afternoon. A Kanto bus leaves for Ohira-san from in front of Tochigi Station and reaches the foot of the mountain in about 15 minutes.

Near the bus terminus there is a hexagonal building called the Rokkaku-do, and the road going off to the right of this leads via about 700 stone steps to Ohira Shrine, founded in 827 and located near the top of the 343-meter-high mountain. On the way up you pass the shrine's main red gate, erected in 1723, and along the road to the left of this there is a good observation point offering views over Tochigi and the Kanto Plain.

Just to the right of Ohira Shrine there is the starting point for the Iwafune hiking course, leading to Iwafune Station on the Ryomo Line by way of Fuji-Sengen Shrine (just above Ohira Shrine), Mount Teruishi (419 meters) and Mount Umairazu (345 meters). The course takes about three hours to complete. From Iwafune it's 13 minutes by train back to Tochigi.

Ohira Shrine.

In Search of Flowers Around Nikko

日光

IT takes less than 2 hours to reach Nikko by special express on the Tobu Nikko Line from Asakusa, but so rich are the pickings in this tourist mecca of Tochigi Prefecture that at least one night's stay is recommended.

The usual sightseeing course around the town begins with the Sacred Bridge (Shinkyo), followed by nearby Rinnoji Temple with its Sanbutsu-do (Three Buddhas Hall) dating from 1648, Toshogu Shrine, Futarasan Shrine, the mausoleum of Tokugawa Iemitsu and the Treasure Museum, finishing off with a visit to the Nikko Botanical Garden which sprawls along a bank of the Daiya River.

Toshogu Shrine was completed in 1636 after two years of labors by craftsmen and artists from all over Japan. Among its many features are the five-storied pagoda and the famous Yomeimon gate. Futarasan Shrine is said to have been founded in 790 in honor of Priest Shodo who was the first person ever to climb Mount Nantai, one of the highest peaks in the area.

Well-known architecture apart, Nikko is also famous for its scenery and most visitors include a trip to Lake Chuzenji in their itinerary. Lake Chuzenji can be reached in about 50 minutes by bus from Nikko along the twisting Irohazaka Driveway. Upon arrival, most people make first of all for Kegon Waterfall and the elevator down to the waterfall's basin. Next comes a sightseeing boat around the lake, which is particularly colorful in autumn.

Both the town of Nikko and Lake Chuzenji have become tourist spots catering in a large way to group travelers, and have suffered from crowds and commercialism as a consequence. Nevertheless, the former in particular is a place of great historic importance and most people like to visit at least once.

Going a little farther afield, the marshy mountain plateau of Senjogahara offers a splendid hiking course and a chance to see alpine plants and flowers in bloom if you go in the summer months. From Nikko board a Tobu bus to Yudaki Iriguchi, the journey taking about

75 minutes, and from there walk to Yudaki (5 minutes), then to Odashirobashi (30 minutes) and then follow the Senjogahara Shizen Kenkyuro course over the 1,400-meter-high plateau as far as Shobugahama, on the shore of Lake Chuzenji. From there you can return to Nikko by Tobu bus in about one hour.

The scenery along the 5.6-km hiking course is excellent, including the 300-meter-long Ryuzu Waterfall just before you reach Shobugahama, and the flowers are at their best in June and July. The route is open to hikers from April until November. Total walking time is about 2 hours 30 minutes.

Another route is the Kirifuri Kogen hike, and the best months to go are from May until August. From Nikko, take a Tobu bus to Kirifuri Kogen (30 minutes). From there, lifts take you up to a height of 1,576 meters and the start of the hiking course. The course leads over a highland meadow and up to the 1,689-meter-high summit of Mount Maruyama, from where fine views can be had of the whole Kirifuri Kogen area. From Mount Maruyama, the route leads to Happyogahara plateau, and thence down and back to the bus stop by means of a lift. Total walking time is about 2 hours.

There are many Western-style hotels and Japanese *ryokan* in the Nikko area, and these can be booked either at a travel agency prior to departure or through information offices at Nikko Station. The Japan Travel Bureau operates one-day and two-day trips to Nikko.

The following camp sites have tent and bungalow facilities available: Shobugahama Camp Village, call 0288-55-0158; Senjogahara Camp Site, call 0288-55-0165; New Kirifuri Bokujo Camp Site, call 0288-54-1973; Kirifuri Camp Site, call 0288-54-0473. Inquiries should be made in Japanese.

Lake Chuzenji

A Village of
Urban
Architecture
明治村

IT is possible to see everything in the Meiji-mura village in a single day. Others may warn you against this but it is possible, I assure you.

To achieve the feat, you have to start early. Try and be at the gates when they open at 10 a.m. If you can't manage this, at least aim to be on the 9:40 direct train from Shin-Nagoya Station to Meiji-mura Guchi Station on the Meitetsu Line, thereby avoiding the usual change at Inuyama. Buses run regularly between Meiji-mura Guchi Station and the village.

If you're lucky enough to be handed a map of the village by a guide on the train, as I was, it's worth using the 35-minute ride to plan a course. Otherwise it's like entering an unfamiliar town without a map, and with the added problem that instead of having just one or two landmarks, Meiji-mura has more than 50.

I don't know whether the founder of the village museum, Dr. Yoshiro Taniguchi (1904-1979), envisioned such a vast park when he originally decided to preserve the finest examples of Japanese Meiji-Period architecture or not, but it certainly is a mammoth display.

Starting with the Meiji-Era main gate itself, inside you have the

Mie Prefectural Normal School and St. John's Church, followed by the Mie Prefectural Office, the Sapporo Telephone Exchange, a gymnasium, Nagoya Garrison Hospital, Kanazawa Prison, a bathhouse, and steam railway and tram services to help you around all the other delights.

Buildings moved to the park from Tokyo include the Shinbashi Railway Factory, the main entrance hall and lobby of the Imperial Hotel, a police box from Tokyo Station, the entrance porch of Tokyo School for the Blind, and an annex of the Imperial Guard Headquarters of the Imperial Palace.

There's so much to see, you probably won't notice the hunger pangs until about 3 in the afternoon. A quick meal will help you over the final stretches of the park as closing time (5 p.m. from March to October, 4 p.m. from November to February) approaches. Be careful, because the only restaurant is located in the northernmost part of the village.

Any complaints? Only that I missed my tram ride because the service stopped too early, and I had to dash to see Shinagawa Lighthouse in the dying seconds before closing time.

Admission fees are ¥1,000 for adults, ¥900 for high schoolers and ¥500 for children through junior high.

A Rocky Ride Over the Kiso Rapids

日本ライン

IT didn't look hopeful. With rain lashing the windows of the train as it left Nagoya, there could be little hope for old wooden boats out on the Kiso River. Or so we thought.

At Inuyama Station, we almost changed our plans and headed for nearby Meiji-mura instead. But figuring that would be equally pointless in the rain, we boarded the train for Nippon Rhine Imawatari as scheduled, and from that station walked to Ota Bridge from where boats leave to descend the Kiso Rapids.

The sight to greet us was one of several boats being punted away from their starting points by boatsmen at front and rear, with blue covers pulled over to protect their passengers from the still driving rain. The Kiso Rapids descent is operated all the year round, with covers used on rainy days and heating installed in winter. The only time the boats are canceled is when the river becomes too swollen and therefore too dangerous.

So we paid our ¥2,400 fees at the Nippon Rhine Center, and then browsed through the souvenirs until our names were called. Boats leave pretty regularly, at 9:30, 10, 11 and 12 in the morning, and at 1, 2 and 3 in the afternoon, the number of vessels depending on demand, with each boat carrying about 20 passengers. Even on a rainy day, the arrival of several busloads of tourist groups ensures that the boatsmen are kept busy.

When your name is called, go down to the riverside and board your boat; the best position from which to view the rapids, the surrounding scenery, and the boatsman as he propels the boat along is at or near the front. A place in the rear is second best.

The total distance of the course is about 13 km, and the journey takes about 80 minutes. The rapids — and shrieks, screams, pale faces and laughter — start about 4 km out. It's wise to take a vinyl sheet along to protect yourself from the spray, even on a fine day.

The name "Nippon Rhine" comes from the fact that the scenery resembles that along the river of the same name in Germany. Certainly the many rocks standing out on both sides of the river present fascinating sights, as suggested by their names: Camel Rock, Lion Rock, Turtle Rock, Spectacles Rock and so on.

Midway along the course are the Kannon Rapids, the most

Shooting the Kiso Rapids (left). Passengers under cover on a rainy day (center), while the boatsman takes a rest (right).

turbulent, and from there you'll also spot the park and shrine of Momo Taro, the peach boy of folk tale fame.

The boat finally comes to rest just before Inuyama Bridge, and on the final stretch you should be able to see Inuyama Castle sitting high on a hill on the other side. Most of the castle was destroyed in the Meiji Period, but the *donjon,* built in 1537, remains the oldest structure of its kind in Japan.

Inuyama Castle is easily reached from the boat's terminus, and it is well worth struggling up the steep donjon stairs not only to see the interior of the structure, but also for the view from the top.

If you're visiting for a weekend and have time to spare after the rapids, the castle, and the famous Meiji-mura, other places which might be of interest in the area include the Japan Monkey Park, Momo Taro amusement park and shrine, and Inuyama Narita-san Temple. These are all within walking distance of Inuyama Yuen Station, one stop from Inuyama.

Two famous fertility festivals, or *honen matsuri*, take place in March. One of them, dedicated to the female sex, is held at Oagata Shrine in Inuyama on the 13th, and the other, dedicated to males, is held at Tagata Shrine in Komaki City, on the 15th. It is wise, they say, to honor the gods by dropping in on both events.

Journey's end.

TRANSPORTATION INDEX

For Around Tokyo Vol. 1 and Vol. 2
Numerals in italics denote pages in Around Tokyo Vol. 1.

119

KEIHIN TOHOKU / NEGISHI LINE STATIONS

Omiya
  Omiya Hikawa Shrine *64, 150*

Kawaguchi
  Kawaguchi Municipal Green Center 102

Akabane
  Akabane Baka Matsuri *143*

Oji
  Oji Inari Shrine *142*, Oji Shrine *150*

Ueno
  See Yamanote Line

Tokyo
  See Yamanote Line

Shinagawa
  See Yamanote Line

Oimachi
  Oi Bird Park *21*

Omori
  Oi Bird Park *21*

Yokohama
  Yokohama Walking Courses *74-79*

Kannai
  Yamashita Park *76, 146*

Ishikawacho
  Jiro Osaragi Memorial Museum *74*

Negishi
  Sankeien *12*

Ofuna
  Yokohama Dreamland *60*, Taya Caves *97*, Ofuna Kannon *97*

YOKOSUKA LINE STATIONS

Ofuna
  See Keihin Tohoku Line

Kamakura
  Kamakura Walking course *80*, Choshoji Temple *142*, Tsurugaoka Hachimangu Shrine *143, 147, 81*, Zeniarai Benten Shrine *81*, 81

Zushi
  Aburatsubo *106*, Jogashima *107*

Yokosuka
  Aburatsubo *106*, Jogashima *107*

Kurihama
Aburatsubo *106*, Jogashima *107*

TOKAIDO LINE STATIONS

Tokyo
See Yamanote Line

Yokohama
See Keihin Tohoku Line

Odawara
Odawara Castle *85*, Oshiro Matsuri *144*, Mt. Akiba *150*, Old Hakone Road 27, Hakone Walking Course 29

Atami
MOA Art Museum 95, Hatsushima 95

TOKAIDO SHINKANSEN STATIONS

Tokyo
See Yamanote Line

Odawara
See Tokaido Line

Shizuoka
Kunozan Hill 100, Kunozan Toshogu Shrine 100, Nihondaira Plateau 100

Mishima
Mt. Fuji *102*

Nagoya
Meiji-mura Village (Meitetsu Line) 114

IZU KYUKO RAILWAY

Ito
Izu Cactus Park 96, Hatsushima 96, Jogasaki Picnical Course 96, Mt. Komuro Park 97

Izu Kogen
Jogasaki Shizen Kenkyuro 96, Jogasaki Bunka Shiryokan 97

Izu Atagawa
Atagawa Banana and Alligator Park 97

Izukyu Shimoda
Shimoda Walking Course 92, 97, Cape Irozaki 97, Irozaki Jungle Park 97

MINOBU LINE STATION

Fujinomiya
Mt. Fuji 101

121

SOBU LINE STATIONS

Chiba
Kasori Shell Mound *37*

Ichikawa
Satomi Park *83*

Koiwa
Zenyoji Rose and Azalea Fair 55

Kinshicho
Nose Myokenzan Betsuin Temple *142*

Ryogoku
Earthquake Memorial Museum *26*

SOBU MAIN LINE STATION

Choshi
Mt. Atago 87, Byobugaura 87

UCHIBO LINE STATIONS

Sanukimachi
Mother Farm *52*

Hama Kanaya
Mt. Nokogiri 35, Nihonji Temple 36

SOTOBO LINE STATION

Katsuura
Katsuura Walking Course 89, Katsuura Kaichu Koen 89

JOBAN LINE STATIONS

Kameari
Towa Ginza Shotengai Market 73

Kanamachi
Mizumoto Park *144,* Shibamata Ground *146*

Tsuchiura
Mt. Tsukuba 40

NARITA LINE STATION

Narita
Narita Shinshoji Temple 85

MOKA LINE STATION

Mashiko
    Mashiko Fair 70, Togei no Mori 70

CHUO LINE STATIONS

Tokyo
    See Yamanote Line

Ochanomizu
    Nicolai Cathedral *69*, Meiji Univ. Penal Museum *130*, Kanda Myojin Shrine *141, 144*

Iidabashi
    Koishikawa Korakuen *2*, Michio Miyagi Memorial Hall *120*

Shinjuku
    See Yamanote Line

Koenji
    Awa Odori *147*

Asagaya
    Tanabata Matsuri *146*

Ogikubo
    Zenpukuji Park *17*, Igusa Hachiman Shrine *148*

Nishi Ogikubo
    Zenpukuji Park *17*, Morning Market 72

Kichijoji
    Inokashira Park *17, 143*, Zenpukuji Park *17*

Hino
    Takahata Fudo Temple *66*

Hachioji
    Mt. Takao *99, 142, 149*, 2

Fujino
    Fujino Engei Land 24

Matsumoto
    Matsumoto Course 108, Azumino 108, Utsukushigahara Plateau 108

FUJI KYUKO LINE STATION

Kawaguchiko
    Mt. Fuji 101

OME LINE STATIONS

Ome
    Ome Daruma Fair *141*, Ome Railway Park *39*

Private Lines

ODAKYU LINE STATIONS

Mukogaoka Yuen
Mukogaoka Yuen Amusement Ground *59*, Nihon Minkaen *28*

Yomiuri Land-mae
Yomiuri Land Amusement Ground *60*

Machida
Machida Iseki Park *35*

Odakyu Sagamihara
Sagami River Otako-age *144*

Isehara
Mt. Oyama *31*

Ohatano
Mt. Oyama *31*

Odawara
See Tokaido Line

ODAKYU ENOSHIMA LINE STATION

Katase Enoshima
Enoshima Walking Course *104*

ENODEN LINE STATIONS

Katase Enoshima
See Odakyu Enoshima Line

Shonan Kaigan Koen
Enoshima Aquarium and Marineland *104*, *80*

Hase
Hase Kannon *81*, Kamakura Daibutsu *81*

Kamakura
See Yokosuka Line

HAKONE YUMOTO TOZAN LINE STATION

Chokoku no Mori
Hakone Open Air Museum *46*

KEIO LINE STATIONS

Shinjuku
See Yamanote Line

Roka Koen
Roka Park *24*

Tsutsujigaoka
Jindai Botanical Garden *144*, *149*, *78*, Jindaiji Temple *142*

Chofu
Fuda Tenjin Shrine 62, Jindai Botanical Garden *144, 149,* 78

Fuchu
Okunitama Shrine 64, Sumomo Plum Festival 64, Kurayami Darkness Festival 64, Kuri Chestnut Festival 64

Keio Hachioji
Mt. Takao *99, 142, 149,* 2, Mt. Jinba 3

KEIO SAGAMIHARA LINE STATION

Keiotamagawa
Keio Hyakkaen *144*

KEIO DOBUTSUEN LINE STATION

Tama Dobutsukoen
Tama Tech *60,* 67, Tama Zoo 67

KEIO TAKAO LINE STATION

Takaosan-guchi
Mt. Takao *99, 142, 149,* 2

KEIO INOKASHIRA LINE STATIONS

Shibuya
See Yamanote Line

Komaba Todaimae
Nihon Mingeikan *131*

Inokashira Koen
Inokashira Park *17, 143*

SEIBU IKEBUKURO LINE STATIONS

Ikebukuro
See Yamanote Line

Sakuradai
Sakuradai Kita-guchi Market 73

Shakujiikoen
Shakujii Park *17*

Hibarigaoka
Heirinji Temple *66*

Hanno
Mt. Tenranzan 14

Agano
Koburi-toge *17*

Shomaru
　　Mt. Izugatake 19, Shomaru-toge 19

SEIBU TOSHIMA LINE STATION

Toshimaen
　　Toshimaen Amusement Ground 59

SEIBU SAYAMA LINE STATION

Seibu Kyujomae
　　UNESCO Village 44

SEIBU SHINJUKU LINE STATIONS

Takadanobaba
　　See Yamanote Line

Araiyakushimae
　　Tetsugakudo Park 6, Araiyakushi Temple 114

Kami Igusa
　　Chihiro Iwasaki Picture Book Museum 131

Higashi Fushimi
　　Musashiseki Park 17

Tanashi
　　Tanashi Market 73

Hana Koganei
　　Koganei Park 33

Honkawagoe
　　Kawagoe Walking Course 68, Daruma Fair 69, Kawagoe Fudo Temple
　　69, Kitain Temple 68, 78

SEIBU HAIJIMA / TAMAKO LINE STATIONS

Haijima
　　Daruma Fair 78

Seibu Yuenchi
　　Seibuen 59

CHICHIBU DENTETSU RAILWAY STATIONS

Nagatoro
　　Nagatoro 93

Chichibu
　　Chichibu Shrine 146, 150

Urayamaguchi
　　Hashitate Cave 12

Mitsumineguchi
Mt. Mitsumine 21

TOKYU TOYOKO LINE STATIONS

Shibuya
See Yamanote Line

Yutenji
Yutenji Market 73

Gakugeidaigaku
Himonya Park *16*

TOKYU SHIN-TAMAGAWA LINE STATIONS

Sangenjaya
Sangenjaya Market 72

Futakotamagawa
Okamoto Minkaen *71,* Futakotamagawaen Amusement Ground *59*

Nagatsuda
Kodomo no Kuni 80

TOKYU IKEGAMI LINE STATIONS

Senzokuike
Senzoku Pond *17*

Ikegami
Ikegami Honmonji Temple *141, 146, 148,* 54

TOKYU MEKAMA LINE STATIONS

Fudomae
Meguro Fudo 56

Shimomaruko
Shimomaruko Market 73

Yaguchi no Watashi
Yasukata Shotengai Market 73

KEIHINKYUKO KURIHAMA LINE STATIONS

Shinagawa
See Yamanote Line

Yokosuka Chuo
Mikasa Park *72*

Miura Kaigan
Cape Kenzaki 33

KEIHINKYUKO MAIN LINE STATION

Uraga
   Kannonzaki Park *18*

KEIHINKYUKO DAISHI LINE STATION

Kawasaki Daishi
   Kawasaki Daishi Temple *151*, 61

TOKYO MONORAIL LINE STATION

Ryutsusenta
   Oi Bird Park 21

SOTETSU LINE STATIONS

Yokohama
   See Keihin Tohoku Line

Futamatagawa
   Makigahara Children's Park *54*

TOBU ISESAKI / NIKKO LINE STATIONS

Asakusa
   Asakusa Kannon Temple *141, 145, 149, 151,* Asakusa Sengen Shrine
   144, 145, Asakusa Shrine *144,* Torigoe Shrine *141, 145,* O-Fuji-San
   Plant Fair 55

Tamanoi
   Mukojima Hyakkaen *4*

Tobu Dobutsu Koen
   Tobu Zoo *56*

Tochigi
   Tsukada Museum 110, Ohira Shrine 111, Iwafune Hiking Course 111

Nikko
   Toshogu Shrine 112, Lake Chuzenji 112, Senjogahara Hiking Course
   112, Kirifuri Kogen Hiking Course 113

TOBU TOJO LINE STATIONS

Ikebukuro
   See Yamanote Line

Kami Itabashi
   Kami Itabashi Market 72

Narimasu
   Akatsuka Market 73

Shiki
　Heirinji Temple *66*

Kawagoe
　Honda Airport *137*, Kawagoe Walking Course 68, Kitain Temple 68, 78,
　Kawagoe Fudo Temple 69, Kawagoe Festival *148,* 69, Daruma Fair 69

Takasaka
　Kodomo Dobutsu Shizen Koen *55*

Higashi Matsuyama
　Yoshimi Caves *95*

Shinrinkoen
　Musashi Kyuryo Shinrin Koen *15*

TOBU DAISHI LINE STATION

Daishimae
　Nishiarai Daishi Temple 60

TOBU KAMEIDO LINE STATION

Higashi Azuma
　Tachibana Ginza Market 73

KEISEI MAIN LINE STATIONS

Keisei Ueno
　See Yamanote Line

Horikiri Shobuen
　Horikiri Shobuen *144*

Konodai
　Satomi Park *83*

Keisei Narita
　Narita Shinshoji Temple 85

KEISEI CHIBA LINE STATION

Keisei Chiba
　Izumi Shizen Koen *14*

KEISEI KANAMACHI LINE STATION

Shibamata
　Yagiri Ferry 48

ARAKAWA TRAM LINE STATION

Minowa
　Otori Shrine *150,* 75

KOMINATO LINE STATION

Yoro Keikoku
Yoro Keikoku 38

MEITETSU INUYAMA LINE STATIONS

Inuyama
Inuyama Castle 118

Nippon Rhine Imawatari
Kiso Rapids 116

MEITETSU KOMAKI LINE STATIONS

Inuyama
See Meitetsu Inuyama Line

Meiji-mura Guchi
Meiji-mura Village 114

GINZA SUBWAY LINE STATIONS

Asakusa
See Tobu Isesaki/Nikko Line

Inaricho
Akiba Shrine *149*

Ueno
See Yamanote Line

Nihonbashi
Kite Museum *122*

Shinbashi
See Yamanote Line

Toranomon
Kasumigaseki Building *136*, Konpira-san Plant Fair 55

Akasaka Mitsuke
Akasaka Mitsuke Boating *16*, Hie Shrine *145*

Shibuya
See Yamanote Line

MARUNOUCHI SUBWAY LINE STATIONS

Ikebukuro
See Yamanote Line

Korakuen
Korakuen *59*

Ochanomizu
See Chuo Line

Otemachi
Communications Museum *131*

Akasaka Mitsuke
See Ginza Subway Line

Shinjuku Gyoenmae
Shojuin Temple *142*, Shinjuku Gyoen National Garden *149*

Higashi Koenji
Myohoji Temple *141*, 58

HIBIYA SUBWAY LINE STATIONS

Minowa
See Arakawa Tram Line

Iriya
Kishibojin Temple *145, 148*

Ueno
See Yamanote Line

Ningyocho
Suitengu Shrine *146, 150*

Tsukiji
Tsukiji Fish Market *116*, Tsukiji Honganji Temple *68*

Hibiya
Hibiya Park *149*

Kamiyacho
NHK Broadcasting Museum *130*

TOZAI SUBWAY LINE STATIONS

Takadanobaba
See Yamanote Line

Waseda
Anahachiman Shrine *147*, Toyama Park *148*, Waseda Univ. Tsubouchi
Memorial Theater Museum *131*

Kudanshita
Yasukuni Shrine *140, 143, 145, 148*, Chidorigafuchi *16*

Takebashi
Chidorigafuchi *16*

Monzennakacho
Tomioka Hachimangu Shrine *146*, Museum of Maritime Science *130*,
Monzennakacho Fairs *46*

CHIYODA SUBWAY LINE STATIONS

TOEI MITA SUBWAY LINE STATIONS

TOEI ASAKUSA SUBWAY LINE STATIONS

GENERAL INDEX

For Around Tokyo Vol. 1 and Vol. 2

Numerals in italics denote pages in Around Tokyo Vol. 1.

135

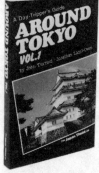